I NEVER
KNEW THAT
ABOUT COLORADO

Library of Congress Cataloging - Publication Data

Fay, Abbott
        I Never Knew That About Colorado
        Included index
        1. Colorado History   I. Title

Library of Congress Catalog Card Number: 97-61804

1997, 1998, 1999, 2001, 2003, 2004
Seventh Edition
Printed in the United States of America

ISBN 1-890437-17-4

Western Reflections Publishing Company®
219 Main St.
Montrose, CO 81401
www.westernreflectionspub.com

I NEVER KNEW THAT ABOUT COLORADO

A Quaint Volume of Forgotten Lore

by Abbott Fay

WESTERN REFLECTIONS PUBLISHING COMPANY®
Montrose, CO

*There is much pleasure
to be gained
from useless knowledge.*

Bertrand Russell

What this is all about

There is no such thing as dead history. True, there may be "dead" historians, "dead" history texts, "dead" history teachers, and even "dead" history students.

Nonetheless, history is based on events drawn from letters, observations, and journals — events which had some important meaning to their writers. It is the task of the historian to try to rediscover the feelings of these people, regardless of whether the incidents reported changed the course of the world.

In a career spanning fifty years of study, teaching and writing Colorado history, I have made notes on either long-forgotten or little-publicized happenings. While this is not essentially a book of trivia, some of the items might be considered trivial. Unless an item is described as questionable, it is the result of cross-documentation to indicate that it really happened beyond a reasonable doubt.

A debt of appreciation must go to so many people and other sources that to include all of them is nearly impossible; the bibliographical entries at the end of the book are an authoritative listing of most of the items.

I hope some pleasure may be derived from browsing through these fringes of Colorado history.

Abbott Fay
Grand Junction, Colorado
1997

Table of Contents

Table of Contents, Continued

Table of Contents, Continued

Table of Contents, Continued

About

Original

Coloradans

Pencil sketch of Anasazi ruins at Mesa Verde by Marti Ottinger

Where the Anasazi Culture Comes To Life

Back to the old grind

While Mesa Verde National Park is probably the best known of the Anasazi (Ancient Ones) prehistoric cultural sites, there are numerous others in the "Four Corners" region, where the states of Arizona, New Mexico and Utah meet Colorado.

One of the finest of these sites is the Anasazi Heritage Center in southwestern Colorado near the town of Dolores. When the Dolores River was dammed to create McPhee Reservoir, it was stipulated that part of the costs had to be earmarked for the preservation of one ancient ruin and an educational center to compensate for the inundation of other ruins. This resulted in a great amount of money being spent to create one of the finest museums in Colorado dedicated to one theme. With the help and guidance of the Smithsonian Institution, which still maintains one wing for traveling exhibits, this center is a state-of-the-art exhibition.

Not only are artifacts beautifully and faithfully displayed but an Anasazi dwelling has been re-created within the museum. Frequently, weavers, corn-grinders and basket-makers are on hand to help visitors engage in the actual processes used by people who disappeared from the region 700 years ago. On a short walk from the museum itself, one can visit the remains of an ancient dwelling, preserved from the rising waters of the lake as it filled. ❖

What Did the Name "Cheyenne" Mean?

A problem with official English only

O ne of the more interesting amendments passed by the
population of Colorado in recent years (but which was
later declared unconstitutional) was one that stated simply
that all official business of the state was to be conducted in
English. It was so broadly worded that it was questionable
whether lawyers may even use Latin terms. Were all those
Spanish, French, German and other names of counties and
rivers to be changed? Would even the name Colorado itself
have to be revised from the Spanish for "red color" or simply
"ruddy?" Great heavens!

Perhaps most puzzling, if one were a purist, would be the
name of Cheyenne County, which was named for the Plains
Indians who roamed Eastern Colorado. The Sioux called these
people Shahiyenna meaning "people who speak another language than ours." That may be the best guess as to the origin
of the name, but French fur traders maintained that when
they asked those people their names, they answered
"Cheyenne," which meant either "I don't understand you" or,
because of initiation marks on their bodies, "cut-arm." To re-
name the county in accordance with the amendment, that
region would now have to be called Don't Speak the Same,
Don't Understand, or Cut-arm County. ❖

Slavery in Colorado After the Civil War

What emancipation?

In the so-called "Reconstruction Era" of American history, much attention was paid to immediate steps by northern states to eliminate the practice of slavery in the Confederate states, in accordance with Lincoln's Emancipation Proclamation and the Thirteenth Amendment to the United States Constitution. That constitutional amendment of 1865 specified that neither slavery nor involuntary servitude, except as punishment for crime, was to exist within the United States "or in any place subject to their jurisdiction."

Of course, Colorado was a territory at that time so it was subject to the jurisdiction of the United States government. However, slavery continued for at least another five years in Colorado. This was slavery of Native Americans.

For decades, Native Americans had been sold to Mexicans and Americans. Kit Carson III was the grandson of the colorful Tom Tobin, famed as the killer of the infamous Espinoza gang leaders, and his Ute slave. Antoine Robidoux, at Fort Uncompahgre near the present site of Delta, used to buy children from the impoverished Utes and sell them in the San Luis Valley. He believed he had thus helped both the Ute family survive and supplied farmers with additional labor. It should be pointed out, however, that this was a pretty mild form of involuntary servitude, with many of the slaves becoming members of the families of their owners, both in spirit and through actual marriage.

One early survey at the time of the Amendment listed about 200 slaves. However, when asked if they wanted their freedom, only six stated a desire to return to their original families. Lafayette Head, Indian Agent and later Lieutenant Governor of Colorado Territory, reported 145 slaves in Conejos and Costilla counties in 1865.

The census of 1870 diplomatically omitted reference to these people as slaves. It was reported that most of them did not have any wish for emancipation, as it would mean being turned away without land, food, or a place to live. They reported, as recorded in the Costilla County record book, that they enjoyed freedom to go anywhere and the right to do as they wished.

Eugene Combs, in his unpublished M. A. thesis for Adams State College in Alamosa (1970), pointed out that Colorado slave owners thought the proclamation referred only to the South and to the Negro, and that southwestern territories were not intended for inclusion. However, during the next decade, all slavery designations officially disappeared in Colorado, New Mexico and Arizona. Whether Native American slaves were turned out into an unfamiliar life is doubtful, although some did return to the tribes of their childhood.

It should be noted that most Indian tribes also practiced slavery, despite a current myth that the practice was introduced by Europeans. These slavery practices went unrecorded, except in the letters of some Indian agents. At least some of the Utes condoned the practice until their removal to reservations in 1881. ❖

Lo, the Poor Indian!

Alexander Pope and David Day

David Day, the frequently irascible editor of the *Solid Muldoon* newspaper in Ouray and later Durango, had little sympathy for the Ute Indians who had been displaced by the miners of the San Juan Mountains.

At that time, in the 1880s, most educated people who had read newspapers were familiar with Alexander Pope's *Essay on Man*, which included the words, "Lo, the poor Indians!" Some writers, borrowing from Rousseau, used the phrase as "Lo, the Noble Savage".

Whenever Day referred to the Native Americans, he used the term "Lo" for them as a mark of derision. Thus, he would make such comments as "Ole Lo was in town last night, drunk as usual."

Dave Day was known far and wide for his caustic wit and embelished stories. Day claimed that among his subscribers was Queen Victoria of England. He also claimed to have been received by Her Majesty while on a tour of Europe. He further vowed he was illiterate when he joined the Union Army during the Civil War, in which he won the Congressional Medal of Honor.

As fate would have it, this man who scorned the Utes was appointed Indian Agent for the Southern Ute Reservation during the second administration of President Cleveland.

He died in 1914. There were many tributes nationwide. After praising his rambunctious life, one editor wrote, "Finally Death ran his icy fingers over the silvered hair and the old man entered the dreamless sleep." Day would have appreciated that style. ❖

Buckskin Charlie's Return to Boulder

An agent's needless fears

It is hard to imagine, in these days, the extent of paternalism exercised by Indian Agents only a few decades ago. While reservations were not prisons, the United States government seemed to regard them as at least carefully-supervised orphanages.

At the Southern Ute Reservation, with its headquarters in Ignacio, Buckskin Charlie was the Utes' principal spokesman and leader at the beginning of the twentieth century. While the Utes had been permitted on rare occasions to leave the reservation, the agent there had misgivings about the corrupting influence of the outside world. Such celebrations as Denver's Festival of Mountain and Plains too often involved alcohol and gambling. Even so, Buckskin Charlie had traveled to Washington, D.C. for the inauguration of President Theodore Roosevelt and had returned with no apparent corruption to his moral well-being. Such forays into the urban world were still disdained by the Bureau of Indian Affairs.

When the city of Boulder wished to celebrate its fiftieth anniversary in 1909, the planners hoped to have on hand a contingent of Southern Utes, some of whom had lived in the area when the town was established. When presented with the invitation, the Indians responded enthusiastically. They were told that, among other delights, they would be able to see a moving picture.

The reservation agent, however, was not very pleased with the prospect. He relented when the Boulder officials promised that they would exercise careful supervision over the Indians and protect them from evil influences.

Boulder did live up to this commitment very well, considering that Boulder contained such "questionable elements" as college students. With Buckskin Charlie, who headed the delegation of sixteen, the Utes enjoyed themselves and were pleased to find the site where Utes had once won a battle against the Arapaho Tribe.

Then came the trip to a movie theater. That was many years before there were talking pictures. It was probably just a fluke but the film shown was "Custer's Last Stand." Others in the audience feared that this movie would incite the Utes to "go on the warpath" and seek what Boulderites insisted on calling "fire water." They would burn the city!

Instead, Buckskin Charlie and his friends understood that the picture show was only "make-believe," and they thoroughly enjoyed the way it ended, with the white men being wiped out.

Before their return to Ignacio, the Indians volunteered to go to Denver and take part in a parade which was to promote the Thanksgiving Day football game between the University of Colorado and the Colorado School of Mines. Their appearance was a success and drew a great crowd to the game. Alas, due to their anxious agent, the Utes never got to see the actual game. He took them back to the reservation and out of harm's way. ❖

"Chief" Ouray and Otto Mears in 1868

There Was No Chief Ouray

And a Ute comment on good manners

Almost every work on Colorado history which includes the role of Ute Indians makes reference to "the good Chief Ouray." He is considered "good" in books written about him by modern non-Native American historians because he had the wisdom to agree to the removal of the Utes from this region without warfare. Some Utes, though, especially in northwestern Colorado, probably thought of him as the Benedict Arnold of their people.

There is a question as to how many Utes Ouray actually represented. There were five bands of that tribe in Colorado, but white military men and politicians liked to deal with Ouray. It was they who designated him as a chief. Ouray was fluent in Spanish and several Indian dialects. He also spoke at least "pidgin" English. Thus, it was Ouray who was chosen by the United States government as the treaty-maker for all Utes. It was Ouray who was sent to Washington, D. C. to become something of a celebrity there.

The Utes never had leaders they regarded as "chiefs." These people were not organized in the same manner as other tribes which the white men had encountered. For instance, plains tribes had to be well-organized for buffalo hunts and they needed a commander. They brought this same formidable structure to the Indian uprisings following the Civil War.

Ute Indians roamed the mountains in extended family groups but did, on occasion, elect a spokesman, called "Avought Datwdtch", for each particular band. These representatives were therefore considered leaders only in a vague sense. Certainly Ouray served that purpose on occasion for the Uncompahgre Utes, his own band, but he probably had no real leadership over the other four groups.

It must be remembered that the Utes of the Mountain West in Colorado saw very few white men. They did not see any such thing as an "iron horse" until shortly before the expulsion of the Utes from their hunting lands. They had no experience with telegraph systems and other devices of nineteenth century invention. It must have been almost laughable for Ouray, returning from Washington, to try to explain that there were millions of White Men, with huge cannons and vast cities, living beyond the Continental Divide. Yet that is what he was sent to the East to discover. It is little wonder that he could not conceive of a resistance to the U. S. government.

Modern Utes on the Uintah and Ouray Reservation in Utah have pointed out that references to Native American men of any tribe as "chief" is considered insulting in much the same way as some whites used to refer to black men as "boy." Alas, there are still many who call their co-workers of Indian heritage "chief," meaning no offense and not realizing the connotation as a racist remark.

It might be added that Ouray himself, who pronounced his name as "You-ray," never seemed to have objected to being called "Chief of all the Utes" and he did not hesitate to sign documents by that title. ❖

Colorow's Big Game Round-up in Middle Park

An ill wind blows no good

In 1878, just before the fateful attack on Nathan C. Meeker, Ute agent for Northwestern Colorado, there was bitter resentment as a result of Meeker's demands that the Utes depend on United States government food supplies rather than hunting on their own. Due to government red tape, the supplies were sometimes held at the railway station in Rawlins, Wyoming. Often, as a result of corrupt contractors, the food received was polluted or the bean sacks filled with many pebbles.

The Utes were so desperate that they even appealed to then Governor Frederick Pitkin for the removal of Meeker. Pitkin was one of those who seemed to be just hoping that something would happen to justify the taking of the Ute Reservations into the White Man's domain.

It was then, during the autumn months, that Colorow, who considered himself a leader of the White River Utes, became disturbed. He felt that the white settlers of

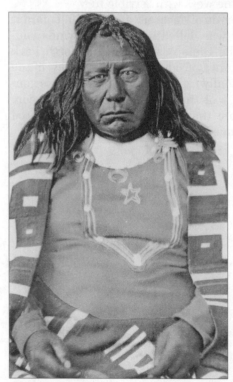

Ute Chief Colorow weighed 300 pounds

Middle Park, near the modern site of Granby, on the edge of
the reservation, were killing too many game animals.

Noting the prevailing westerly winds, Colorow conceived of
the idea to drive wild game into the reservation lands by
means of a gigantic forest and brush fire. The timber and
sagebrush were very dry. He and several companions started
the flames high in the Medicine Bow range, and the conflagration took off toward the west with terrible fury.

The blaze drove the herds of deer, elk and buffalo before it
in a stampede. Colorow was delighted until the winds suddenly shifted, sending the game northward into North Park
and the Wyoming plains, away from Ute territory. A few of the
animals may have eventually returned but that seems to generally have been the last of the buffalo seen in the region.
Many years passed before the forests and ranges recovered
from the devastation wrought by this angry Ute. ❖

ABOUT REMARKABLE FOLKS

A hunter's shack in the Rocky Mountains

Stained Glass Window
Honors Theodore Roosevelt

Shooting big game from a patio

The adventures of Theodore Roosevelt as a bear hunter in Colorado are often cited as one reason for his interest in the West. That interest led to better National Forest regulation and the beginnings of land reclamation in Colorado. The legend holds that after an unsuccessful hunt, the staff of the Colorado Hotel in Glenwood Springs invented a doll known as the "Teddy Bear" to console the President. While the name "Teddy" stuck to the dolls, bear dolls seem to have been produced in Germany for generations before one was made in Glenwood Springs.

Two weeks after he was inaugurated in 1905, Roosevelt came to Colorado for a hunting vacation on Divide Creek, south of the town of Silt. While there, a Rifle minister gave a sermon to the assemblage at the little "Blue School" in that region. Later, the pastor promoted the inclusion of a stained glass window commemorating the Presidential visit. The new Rifle church had a series of beautiful windows. One became known as the Roosevelt Window. When the church was abandoned years later, Rifle citizens pitched in to save the window and placed it in the local library, now a tourist attraction.

Incidentally, Roosevelt was once a guest of John Osgood at his luxurious Cleveholm Manor (now called the Redstone Castle) at Redstone, Colorado. The story has it that Osgood, then president of the Colorado Fuel and Iron Corporation, wanted to do something very special for the famous visitor. Osgood ordered his staff to drive a number of wild animals, including a bear, across the spacious grounds so that Roosevelt could sit on the patio and shoot at them. While that doesn't sound very sportsmanlike, it is possible that "Teddy" went along with it rather than to seem ungracious to his host. ❖

The Doctor Who Made Real House Calls

His mobile home was unique

There are some remarkable mobile home units in the form of luxurious trailers, recreational vehicles, and other conveyances today. However, a physician in the hamlet of Twin Lakes, at the foot of Mt. Elbert, the state's highest peak, had a traveling office which seems to be unique in history.

Twin Lakes was the site of a number of isolated mines and some ranching, located not far from booming Leadville.

A little booklet published in that town in 1943 carried the reminiscences of Patrick J. Ryan, who was one of the earliest pioneers of Twin Lakes. Among his accounts was his memory of one "Old Dr. Rice." Rice traveled in a sleigh to call on his far-flung patients during the winter of 1882.

The good doctor had built a house on the sleigh framework, complete with a small stove and a little crooked stovepipe sticking out of the roof. Driving the horse from an opening in front, he could make his visits in fine comfort. There was room in the "sleigh-house" for an ample supply of wood to keep the home fires burning while he tended the needs of his patients. This puts a somewhat different slant on the term "house calls." ❖

How Stanley Got to Africa

Finding Ouray before finding Livingston

Henry Stanley, who became world-famous for finding Dr. Livingston in Africa, spent considerable time exploring the West before the time of that adventure. As a reporter for the *St. Louis Democrat*, he traveled in Colorado. On one occasion he took a twelve-foot skiff, loaded with provisions, down the Platte River, then the Missouri River, from Denver to St. Louis.

Among Stanley's friends was Col. Lewis N. Tappan. Tappan was the founder of the first Sunday school in Colorado. He had criticized Professor Oscar Goldrick, Denver's first schoolmaster, for conducting school seven days a week, thereby violating the Sabbath. As a result, Goldrick reformed and the students were sent to church school on Sundays.

Stanley asked to go along when the respected Col. Tappan was sent to the San Juans of southwestern Colorado to meet "Chief" Ouray and negotiate the agreement whereby miners could enter and settle on what had been land reserved forever to the Ute Indians. As a result of the mutual respect the two gained, Tappan was able to write a strong recommendation for Stanley to the *New York Herald*, which sponsored the famed search for Livingston. Stanley later reported to Tappan that it was that recommendation, detailing the imagination, tenacity, and sense of adventure of the reporter, which moved the editor in New York to send Stanley to Africa. ❖

Some Middle-Aged Men
Shouldn't Have Gone West

How Meeker messed up

Horace Greeley seems to have been stuck with having given the advice to "Go West, young man, go West!" He denied time and again that he was the originator of the remark but folklore is a powerful force. It is true that he did write it, quoting John Babsome Lane Soul's article in the Terre Haute *Indiana Express* in 1851. Actually, when Greeley himself came West, he had very little that was favorable to say about it.

Unfortunately, Greeley's famous advice was picked up and publicized by Nathan C. Meeker, Greeley's agricultural editor on the *New York Tribune*. Meeker made a huge mistake all the way around by following that admonition.

Meeker lured farmers to his Union Colony (now the city of Greeley) which was a socialistic failure under his

Nathan Meeker had high hopes

leadership. When the colony failed to conform to his authoritarian demands, he decided that it was corruption in the modern civilization that was to blame.

Meeker also longed to teach the "noble savage" how to live. Thus, he was able to get himself appointed as the agent for the White River Ute Indians, in northwestern Colorado. He imme-

diately foisted his arrogance upon the Utes, insisting that
they call him "Father Meeker." He forbade them to go hunting and refused to issue rifles and ammunition, despite the
lack of delivery of federal foodstuffs. When food did arrive,
much of it was spoiled.

Gradually Meeker lost control and sent for federal troops.
At last, when he ordered the Ute men to tear up their
horseracing track and plant potatoes, they sent a delegation
to Denver to have him removed. When that failed, the Utes
ended his career by driving a stake through his heart. ❖

The Meeker Massacre Site

Elks Lodge Founder Died in Leadville

The Jolly Corks of the Cloud City

Charles Algernon Sidney Vivian, son of an English clergy-man, migrated to the United States in 1867. He became a variety actor and ballad singer, touring the country with various performing companies.

In the old country, Vivian had been a member of an organization of actors and other stage personalities called the "Buffaloes." This club was established partly for mutual camaraderie and also as a sort of insurance plan for members down on their luck. In New York, he organized an American counterpart for this order, calling it the "Jolly Corks."

Later, the Jolly Corks became infatuated with a fine, mounted elk head displayed in P.T. Barnum's famous New York museum. They promptly re-named themselves the Benevolent and Protective Order of Elks. It was noted by them that the elk was "fleet of foot, timorous of doing wrong, avoiding all combat save in the defense of its young, the helpless and the weak."

In 1879, Vivian came to Leadville as a member of the famous Jack Langrishe troupe of performers. He stayed to produce his own version of *Oliver Twist* but the play didn't do well. After that he did solo acts in various places around the booming mining camp. When Vivian and his wife could not find suitable housing, Eddie Foy, another famous actor, came to the rescue, sharing his home with them.

Some of their performances were given at the famous Tabor Opera House in what had by then become Colorado's second largest city, Leadville. Soon, he enlisted men to join Chapter 236 of the Elks Lodge, one of only a few begun by the founder of the order himself.

In January of 1880, the city was swept with an outbreak of pneumonia. With Leadville's altitude of nearly two miles, any respiratory illness was often fatal. Vivian fell victim and died in March of that year.

Buried with great ceremony in Leadville's Evergreen Cemetery, he was memorialized with the band playing his favorite song, "Ten Thousand Miles Away." He had frequently received ovations for his performance of that song, which he felt represented the distance from his birthplace. Concert halls put on benefits for his widow, soon raising enough money for her return to the East. Vivian's body was disinterred nine years later and moved to the Elks' Cemetery in Boston.

Leadville Elks bought the Tabor Opera House and preserved it from the fate of Denver's larger version which was built by H.A.W. Tabor. The Leadville building was subsequently purchased by a private party and has been maintained as a museum. It is used only occasionally for performances. The Denver Tabor Opera House was destroyed, along with the old Mining Exchange Building (former Denver Post Office, built on Tabor's donated property) in order to construct the Brooks and Executive Tower buildings. ❖

The Blind Poet of the San Juan Mountains

The Milton of Colorado

Perhaps he was a minor poet in the annals of Colorado history, but certainly his work was a tribute to the beauty of the San Juan mountains which he could no longer see when he wrote about them.

Alfred Castner King was only sixteen years of age when he went to work in the mines at Ouray. Born in Michigan, his family had ended up living on the Western Slope. Alfred was a very talented young man, having written compositions as early as the age of eight. In 1900, at the age of twenty-six, he was blinded as a result of the explosion of three boxes of dynamite caps in the mine.

In spite of his injuries, his fiance married him, and they embarked on a career with the Chautauqua circuit, playing the flute and lecturing. He wrote numerous poems, and some were published as books: *Mountain Idylls* and *The Passing of the Storm*. He was able to market his delightful poetry at these lectures.

In the epic poem, "The Passing of the Storm," which gave the title to his second book, he related the plight of some miners caught in an avalanche and how they really discovered each other while trapped in a small cabin.

One editor called King the "Milton of Colorado - the Blind Poet of Ouray." It was said that he could recite forty to fifty pages of poetry at a time from memory. He lived most of his life in that mountain town and died at Grand Junction in 1941. ❖

Mr. Hershey's Candy Bar Conceived in Denver

The secret was fresh milk

When apprentice confectioner Milton Hershey accompanied his father from Pennsylvania to Denver during the 1880s, the young man went to work for a local candy-maker. His father, Henry, had come West hoping to cash in on the booming silver market but came out a loser.

However, while in the Queen City, Milton realized that fresh milk could make a better chocolate which held its texture and flavor longer than the traditional methods. Back in those days, chocolate was an expensive candy which only the well-to-do could really afford. It has been said that Hershey was to chocolate candy what Henry Ford was to the automobile. Back in the Mennonite region of his home state, Milton eventually produced the famous inexpensive Hershey candy bar in a town which was named for him and had streets named for the ingredients of the famous bar. With mass production, the rich milk chocolate candy became affordable to the masses.

In his eighties, Hershey produced the famous long-lasting tropical chocolate during World War II. As a part of combat "D-rations," it became a world-wide favorite, both for the American servicemen and as the most popular gift to war refugee children. He simply extended the thinking he had first realized in Denver. ❖

Jim Bridger's Struggle
With William Shakespeare

The Bard had a mean streak

The famous frontiersman, Jim Bridger, served as guide to Sir St. George Gore's infamous poaching expedition into what is now northern Colorado in 1857. There were more animals slaughtered on this safari than any other known in the Rockies.

When Bridger, who was illiterate, became a close friend of his boss, he asked Gore what he felt the best books were. Among them, Gore mentioned Shakespeare. Bridger met a wagon train of emigrants in southern Wyoming and traded a yoke of cattle to them for a book of Shakespeare's works. He then hired a German boy to read the plays to him.

While he enjoyed the works, he became, sometimes, infuriated with the bard. The murder of two princes in the Tower of London upset him, and he decided Shakespeare must have had a mean streak to have "written such scoundrelism as that."

At any rate, he did memorize some quotes from the works, and used them, with his own spicy variations from time to time, giving the impression that Shakespeare himself had used those "mule-skinner" expressions.

Two observers at the time recorded these explorations into Shakespeare's famous works. One was R. B. Marcy, in *Thirty Years of Army Life,* and the other was from letters received by Margaret Carrington in her *Ab-Sa-Ra-Ka, Land of the Massacre.* ❖

Laura Evans' Morality Lecture

Prostitution vindicated

One of the more famous of Colorado's "Madams" in the days of legal or semi-legal prostitution, and perhaps a little beyond that era, was Laura Evans of Salida. For more than a half century, she ran a sporting house on Front Street in that town.

Laura lived to the age of ninety. Shortly before her passing in 1953, she was the subject of several interviews about her illustrious career.

In one of these interviews, she lamented that the public attitude toward prostitution was woefully false. Prostitution, she maintained, had probably prevented many rapes and other atrocities throughout the period of Colorado history when there was a shortage of women to satisfy the carnal needs of the men. "If they want it, they should pay for it!" she exclaimed.

The practice served a useful purpose even later, Laura went on to say, by preserving the morals of young ladies who chose to remain chaste until marriage. The Madam predicted that in future years, men would take advantage of their girl friends before marriage and that unmarried sex would become commonplace.

It is said that her funeral was one of the best attended in Salida history and included many ladies who had never met Laura. ❖

Rattlesnake Kate

Gathering dress material

Only a few maps show the village of Ione in these days. It was located about halfway between Fort Lupton and Platteville in what is now called the Four Way area.

Katherine Slaughterback owned a homestead a bit east of Ione, on which there was a small pond. On October 28, 1925, she had a singular adventure which was later described by historical writer Frances Melrose.

It seems that there were some duck hunters at the pond, and she was sure that they had wounded some fowls which they had not recovered. Kate was not wealthy, and the prospect of finding some ducks was well worth the effort of searching. She went out to the pond with her shotgun and her three-year-old son, Eric.

As they trod down the path, they were suddenly confronted by a rattlesnake. Kate shot it but suddenly realized there were a dozen more near at hand. She soon ran out of shells, and still more snakes appeared!

Kate ripped off a "No Hunting" sign and used the post to begin clubbing the snakes. It took her two hours to kill what reporters claimed were 140 rattlers.

The bodies were not wasted. Kate skinned them and pieced them together to make a dress for herself.

When she died in 1969, Katherine Slaughterback was interred at Platteville, where the inscription on her tombstone reads "Rattlesnake Kate."   ❖

The Guardians of St. Elmo

No lookers, only buyers

One of the better-preserved "ghost towns" in Colorado has been St. Elmo, on Chalk Creek above Nathrop. A booming town in 1880, this mining camp between Mount Princeton and Mount Antero was named for the novel, *Saint Elmo*, a best-seller of the last century by Augusta Evans Wilson. By 1922, the last mine there had closed, but Annabel and Tony Stark, sister and brother, stayed on, running the tiny general store and post office.

When this writer first visited St. Elmo in 1952, we parked in front of the store to look around. Out ran Annabel, who told us to get moving as no one was wanted there. We said we had come to buy something, and the tone changed. As we entered the store, she quickly put on lipstick. Then she sold us each a candy bar, for fifteen cents apiece when they were universally sold for a nickel. Anyway, that changed the atmosphere, and she showed us around "her town."

It was in great condition. This was the era of souvenir hunters who damaged so many old mining and ranching towns in Colorado. It was, without a doubt, preserved by the possessive attitude of the Starks. She told us that a woman artist had come and drawn pictures and "made a million dollars from a book" but had never shared it with the Starks. (We later determined that she was referring to the highly-respected Muriel Sibell Wolle, whose *Stampede to Timberline* certainly did not net that fantastic sum, although St. Elmo was well-mentioned in the work.)

A few years later, Tony and Annabel passed on. A number of people purchased the buildings there as summer homes and maintained them, holding to the spirit of the Starks. The town has remained relatively unvandalized as a result. ❖

How Nucla Conquered The Nation

The buccaneer of land reform

The town of Nucla, in western Montrose County, was founded as a Utopian farming community at the beginning of the twentieth century. It was based on socialism, pure and simple. Citizens were dedicated to such ideas as subsidizing crop production, sharing the wealth, and taxation of the rich to help out the poor. These ideas were considered on the level of Bolshevism at that time, and when missionaries of the idea distributed brochures in Montrose to promote the radical concepts, most people were shocked.

James Patton took Nucla's experiment to Washington

James Patton's father moved to Nucla shortly after the birth of his son, and the lad grew up with these ideals. Gradually, however, the Nucla experiments failed, one by one. After going to Grand Junction for a high school education, Patton took a degree at Western State College in Gunnison and became a teacher. During the depths of the Great Depression, he sold insurance for the Colorado Farmers' Union and gradually worked up in that organization to become president.

It was not long before his leadership abilities made him the president of the National Farmers' Union, and he was re-elected unanimously fifteen times to that position, becoming the leader of a voting block of well over a million farmers under his guidance. Patton gradually became the so-called "Buccaneer of Land Reform," being consulted by the Department of Agriculture during the Roosevelt "New Deal" years. Many of his drastic ideas, drawn from his Nucla youth, were adapted as national policy — for better or worse. His leadership continued through the Truman administration, and when the Republicans took office, they still retained his concepts and enlarged on some, with his advice. Then came the Kennedy and Johnson administrations, further refining these policies. When Patton finally retired in 1966, the ideals of Nucla, long forgotten there, had not only been realized but were extended beyond what had been envisioned by the pioneers of that radical movement. ❖

Last Widow of a Slave and Civil War Veteran

Poet and writer Daisy Anderson

D aisy Anderson died Sept. 26, 1998 at a Denver nursing home. She is believed to have been the last surviving widow of a former slave and veteran of the War Between the States.

Daisy lived in Colorado for more than half a century. A native of Arkansas, at the age of twenty-two she married Robert Anderson, seventy-nine, in 1922. He had been born into slavery, and later, with his master's permission, joined the Union Army late in the Civil War.

After serving with the military on the Great Plains during the Indian unrest, he made several attempts to build a career. He finally took a homestead near Hemmingford, Nebraska, where he built his own sod house and eventually became a wealthy rancher. He traveled extensively, throughout the United States, Cuba and Mexico.

On one of his visits to the South, Robert came to the conclusion that he was in need of a companion in his old age. He married Daisy Graham, of Forest City, Arkansas, bringing her to his Nebraska ranch as a partner.

Although she was widowed a few years later, young Daisy was able to manage the ranch until the Great Depression of the Thirties, when she lost all the property. She then moved to Colorado to begin a new life, choosing the beautiful Strawberry Park, near Steamboat Springs, as her home.

Before Robert, who was illiterate, died, Daisy had taken meticulous notes on the recollections of his career. She wrote them as a biography, which she published as *From Slavery to Affluence: Memoirs of Robert Anderson, Ex-Slave.*

Daisy was also an accomplished poet, winning several national awards. On one occasion she was honored by some of the stars of show business in New York as one of the great black women of this century.

In later editions of the book, Daisy wrote a poignant essay,

"Have You No Shame?" in which she expressed gratitude for the liberation of slaves but considerable chagrin at the racist attitudes that had made life very difficult for her.

She later added another essay, "Into Every Life Some Rain Must Fall," in which she commented, "This is a beautiful area; most people have changed; the laws of the State of Colorado have changed. One seldom sees people with a cruel attitude that some people had when I came here. We all have learned a lesson - it is to welcome all people who come to this area." She then dedicated her works to the people of Steamboat Springs and Routt County, who had overcome the racial prejudice which had existed when she first came to Colorado. ❖

A typical Civil War scene.

Physician, Take Out Thine Own Appendix!

Was it done with mirrors?

One of the most unusual cases in Colorado medical history must have been that of Dr. George C. Balderson, a doctor who removed his own appendix.

Balderson, who grew up in the beautiful fruit-producing Colorado town of Paonia, was a very innovative person. When he was practicing medicine in Telluride in 1940, he had an attack of appendicitis. He decided to remove the appendix himself, with a nurse in attendance. (Some accounts claim he did consent to have another physician view the operation.)

In spite of the fact that such an operation was considered very serious surgery in those days, Balderson was up and seeing patients within two days.

After a World War II stint in the Navy, he returned to practice in Telluride. In 1949 he moved to Montrose, where he was instrumental in developing a large modern hospital facility. Balderson also served for a while as the coroner for Montrose County.

He was so highly respected by his colleagues in Montrose that after he died, in 1979, the annual George C. Balderson Memorial Lectures were instituted in his memory. ❖

A Telluride Banker
Saved His Town by Swindling

A "seedy" hick bilked Manhattan

Charles Delos Waggoner is still hailed as a hero who gave up his own personal liberty to save the people of Telluride during the stock market crash of 1929. A plaque on the main street of that town commemorates the maneuvers of this shrewd thief.

Waggoner was a banker who, ahead of actual events, saw that his bank (already on shaky ground with the closing of most of the mines in that San Juan mountain town) was about to collapse. Rather than see his depositors left destitute, he traveled to Denver and, by a series of clever exchanges between the banks there and in New York City, he was able to deposit $500,000 in his home bank, paying off all the holdings held in trust by him.

He amazed Wall Street. The *New York Times* screamed indignation that a "seedy country banker" had bilked some the nation's most powerful and respected financiers in a simple exchange of telegrams. Later captured in Wyoming, he surrendered willingly and was tried and sentenced to fifteen years in prison in New York. However, the judge was so impressed with the "Robin Hood" aspects of this ploy that he arranged parole within three years.

Wagonner never returned to Telluride or to banking. The bank he saved did finally fail in 1934. The hero later showed up in Georgia, in Grand Junction, Colorado, and in Reno, Nevada, where he finally died after several unsuccessful business ventures. ❖

Only One Colorado High School Graduated a Nobel Prize Winner

Libby and the atomic timeclock

Only one high school in this state can boast that among its alumni is a winner of the coveted Nobel Prize. While many Colorado schools can point with distinction to famous athletes, artists, writers or business leaders who graduated from their programs, only the town of Parachute can claim a winner of the world's most famous award.

When Willard Libby graduated from what was then Grand Valley High School in 1926, the small farming community had very limited scientific equipment but apparently at least one very dedicated chemistry teacher. (The town of Grand Valley later reverted to its original name of Parachute and became a center of the short-lived oil shale boom of the 1970s. The high school is now a part of the Garfield County school system.)

Libby went from his farm upbringing in Grand Valley to the University of California and later served on the chemistry faculty at the University of Chicago. There, he devised the concept of radiocarbon dating: the Carbon-14 test, or atomic timeclock. In 1960, he was awarded the Nobel Prize in chemistry. He died in 1980 at the age of seventy-two. ❖

ABOUT FARMERS AND RANCHERS

No USDA office for Silverton

No Crops At All

Agriculturally-challenged Silverton

San Juan County, with its only extant town being Silverton, may be the only county in the United States without an acre of agricultural land. Even some counties which are totally contained within cities usually have some cash crop. If one excludes the idea of forests as agriculture, then this county holds some sort of record.

The town of Silverton is 9,318 feet above sea level. While it is possible to grow a few garden flowers and some root crops in kitchen gardens, the weather puts a hold on commercial agriculture. The average growing days per year between killing frosts number only fourteen.

Established for the mineral which gave it its name, Silverton was for a long time dependent on mining. Here the infamous Bat Masterson was once the town marshall, although his term was brief, as it had been in most towns, because of his inept performance. He was often more of a law-breaker than a law enforcer.

A story which has never been proven relates that a transient and impoverished songwriter was once sitting at a local bar when a distraught woman entered. She asked the barkeep if her husband had been there. When told he had not, she was said to have replied: "If he comes in, tell the S. O. B. there's going to be a hot time in the old town tonight!" The songwriter jotted that remark down and immortalized the statement in a song. ❖

The Yuma Beefeaters

A trial on the Great Plains

Back in the earliest territorial days of Colorado, Yuma County was still a part of Weld County. While many farmers eked out a living on the plains soil, this land was also very inviting to Texas ranchers who grazed their cattle on drives to the Nebraska trailheads of the Union Pacific Railroad.

While the cattle did graze on wild grasslands, they often found the crops of farmers in the area now occupied by the town of Yuma to be very succulent. This was a source of great distress to the farmers but the ranchers paid no heed to their complaints. So, deciding that the laws did not really apply in the wild land, farmers would, from time to time, kill a cow to supplement their diets.

Angry ranchers finally found one farmer eating Texas beef and were able to have him arrested. At the trial, in the village of Yuma, the charges were made and the prosecution was certain its case was made and that the outcome would be in the ranchers' favor.

Entering upon their deliberations, the jury members first polled themselves as to whether any of them had ever partaken of the forbidden meat. All members admitted to at least one theft. In fact, one said he had just finished butchering a stolen cow before reporting for jury duty that morning. A verdict of innocent was returned, much to the disdain of the prosecutor. ❖

Ranchers Strung Barbed Wire, Too

Fencing off public lands

As Homestead laws became more liberal and provided for more land in the 1870s, many farmers came out west and staked their claims on land that was once considered open range by ranchers. Fencing off this farmland to protect the plants from roving cattle herds and buffalo was a critical need on the high plains of eastern Colorado.

Rock and wooden fences were too expensive in an area covered by grassland which was virtually treeless except along the scarce rivers and streams. Thorn hedges required too many years to grow to efficient height. When the windmill was invented, there was sufficient water on the drylands but, until Joseph F. Glidden began to produce barbed wire in 1874, the problem continued.

Many Old West tales explain that ranchers hated the barbed wire strung around these farms, interrupting what they believed to be their own grazing regions. There were incidents of ranch hands deliberately cutting the fence wires to allow the cattle to roam at will.

In due time, though, the ranchers became among the greatest of barbed wire users. By 1877, some six cattle outfits in Colorado had strung fences around two and a half million acres to claim the public lands as their own property. They had set up a system by which every cowboy working the range, and anyone else the cattle barons could control, filed for homesteads to legalize the holdings. ❖

Succulent Fruits and Veggies

Orange apples and Red McClures

While there have been many species of fruit and vegetables which were developed in Colorado, two became nationally famous.

Jesse Frazer, who brought an ox team across the plains to settle in what is now Florence, back in 1859, brought with him saplings of several types of apple trees. In the higher altitude, he experimented with the orchard stock and eventually went back to Missouri for more samples. His greatest success was the Colorado orange apple which had an unusual flavor that became very popular.

At Carbondale, many decades later, Tom McClure experimented for years to develop a more succulent potato. The result was the famous Red McClure. It was, in the early part of the twentieth century, America's gourmet potato.

The Red McClure thrived especially well in the San Luis Valley. Some time afterward, with enthusiastic support from the State of Idaho, the brown Idaho potato took the place of the Red McClure, and now restaurants have to bow to the results of a successful publicity campaign. There are still Coloradans, though, who think the Red McClure is the tastiest potato ever bred. Now, in the San Luis Valley, farmers have resigned themselves to growing brown potatoes.

At Chicago's Columbian Exhibition in 1893, Colorado produce took gold medals in every category entered. For many years Palisade Peaches and Paonia Cherries were designated as such on menus at New York's Waldorf-Astoria Hotel and on ocean liners. These are still special fruits but Colorado never rallied around the flag the way Idaho did.

Two products that still ring the bell around the nation, though, are the Rocky Ford watermelon and cantaloupe. ❖

Music and Back-Scratching

Keep the cows happy

Perhaps the idea that cowboys should sing began when Puccini produced the opera, "Girl of the Golden West," in 1910. He had never been to the Golden West but that did not matter. As soon as movies had sound tracks, they seemed to favor cowboys who could sing well. Two of the most famous were Gene Autrey and Roy Rogers.

Thus, a lot of people believed singing cowboys were fictional. In truth, though, from the earliest days of cattle ranching in Mexico and the West, cowboy songs were more than just recreational activities. One author claimed that a wrangler who couldn't sing might not get hired for the job. Singing to the cattle when herding at night seemed to settle the cattle and prevent a stampede from some other, stranger sound. The doleful little songs assured the cows that all was well.

Cattle could cause another problem. When the first telephone lines were strung from town to town on the eastern plains of Colorado, it was the custom to set up poles across the ranches, instead of around them, as a distinct economy. One of the problems encountered on that treeless prairie was the absolute delight of the cattle in finding those wonderful scratching posts. Often they would scratch too hard, or perhaps too many times, and break down the poles. ❖

Colorado's Oldest Saddle Horse

The healthy meadows up in Burns

While records have not been kept on the age of riding horses in Colorado, the late historian Harry Chrisman nominated Black Kid as a candidate for the oldest horse in Colorado. Black Kid was a horse owned by Frank Benton who lived near the town of Burns up in Eagle County.

Black Kid died shortly before his fortieth birthday. Chrisman reported that the horse would still raise his hoof to shake hands at the age of thirty-eight even though he was badly crippled with rheumatism. A horse of that age would compare to a human life span of over 100 years. Most horses have a longevity of about twenty to thirty years. The age of forty is considered extreme.

However, Black Kid may have been a mere youngster compared to the world's oldest confirmed age for a horse. The *Guiness Book of World Records* maintains that a horse named Old Billy was sixty-two years old when he died in 1822. That was over in foggy old England where one would think rheumatism was quite widespread.

As for bred ponies, the oldest in the United States was confirmed as Trigger, who died at the age of forty-seven, in Whiteside, Missouri. ❖

ABOUT
MILITARY
AFFAIRS

This photo of Camp Hale was taken in 1943

The Other Ski Troops at Camp Hale

The heroic Viking Battalion

At the summit of Tennessee Pass, near Leadville, there stands an impressive monument listing the names of the men of the famed Tenth Mountain Division who were killed during World War II. It is a shocking number, representing a tenth of the division members. This unit had one of the most impressive combat records of the war. These ski troops trained at nearby Camp Hale and have been justly honored in many books and articles.

Beside that monument stands another, erected by the Sons of Norway, to pay tribute to a different skiing unit which had some of its training at Camp Hale. This was the 99th Infantry Battalion, known as the "Viking Battalion" of the Special Forces. Formed at Camp Riley, Minnesota, this group also made a great contribution to victory in Europe.

On the 25th of March, 1945, these men parachuted into Nazi-occupied Norway where they worked with the underground forces to sabotage German installations. They were the first Americans to take part in the liberation of that country on May 8, 1945. ❖

Discipline in Early Colorado Forts

Sadistic officers and miscreant GIs

Movies have often depicted the soldiers who were stationed in western forts to control the local Indians as heroic, brave, and very virtuous, dedicated men.

Usually not shown are the punishments meted out to offenders by often sadistic officers. These included binding and gagging a soldier for days on end when there was no place for solitary confinement; forcing men to march for whole days carrying heavy logs on their shoulders; and making sport of and humiliating errant warriors by forcing them to crawl long distances and to perform demeaning acts.

All these Spartan treatments did not seem to make the men more stalwart, however. At Fort Crawford, on the Uncompahgre River, the soldiers got together and stole a keg of whiskey, put curtains on the barracks windows, and when morning came they were all drunk.

Desertion was remarkably common. At Fort Garland in 1880, when the troops were ordered to go north to subdue the Utes following the massacre at the White River Agency, more than one-third of them deserted.

Some recruits were enamored with reports of discoveries in the gold fields of Colorado. The men of the Seventh Cavalry, probably stationed at Fort Lyon, had, however, a highly organized desertion plan in 1868.

Thirty men were dispatched from that post for a trek of several days. They were provided with adequate arms and provisions. The sergeant marched them out of the fort at a rapid pace for thirty miles. There he halted the men, telling them it was every man for himself from there on. Most headed for the mountains to seek their fortunes. A few returned to the post and told of the desertion. Some of the miscreants were later captured and given severe whippings. Among these several said they had enlisted for adventure and to get transportation to the West. ❖

Colorado's Women Warriors

Including the Death Battalion

Since white inhabitants of early Colorado settlements lived in constant fear that Indians who had been removed from their hunting grounds might return with a vengeance, several of the settlements may have had units such as Grand Junction's Amazons.

These were women who formed a marching unit with mostly wooden rifles and drilled as a sort of "last line of defense" against what they thought might have been Ute Indian attacks. The Amazons appeared in Independence Day parades and apparently met regularly for close-order drills. The thirty or forty ladies in the group made their own uniforms and apparently did possess a few real rifles.

At no time were they ever in combat, and there is doubt that they even participated in any rifle practice. These women were known as an auxiliary unit to Company F of the Colorado State Militia back in the 1880s. Later in that century, the organization seems to have died out with the realization that the area was not to be invaded by the Utes.

A similar group was formed during World War I by the women students at Colorado State Normal School in Gunnison, now known as Western State College. About twenty of these ladies practiced daily, calling themselves, of all things, "The Death Battalion." ❖

The Spoils of War

Colorado gets a mine and a dam

Near Cameo, in Debeque Canyon east of Grand Junction, there is an unique roller-type dam which was started in 1915 as one of the earliest reclamation projects in the West. It was to furnish Colorado River water to the Grand Valley. This innovative structure was designed by German engineers under a contract from the United States government.

As war broke out in Europe in 1914, one of the casualties was a huge roller for the dam. Shipped from Germany the roller was aboard a merchant vessel which was sunk by the British on the Atlantic Ocean. Apparently, a replacement for it was cast in the United States so the dam could be completed.

However, by that time, this nation was also at war with Germany and, inasmuch as we were on the winning side, the Germans were never paid for their engineering and construction work.

Another booty of that war was the molybdenum mine at Climax, which was founded by a German consortium. The Germans were very impressed by the Japanese Samurai swords and the hardness of their steel. Chemists analyzed the content of the steel and found it to contain molybdenum. (Where the medieval Japanese obtained that rare metal has never been learned.)

Being well into the arms race before World War I, Germany was intent upon obtaining a supply of molybdenum and learned it existed on Bartlett Mountain, near Leadville. That is when Max Schott took the leadership in developing the mine at that location atop Fremont Pass. It was taken over by Americans following the war. When World War II came about, Climax was the source of ninety per cent of the world's supply of molybdenum. ❖

Adolf Hitler's Colorado Ranch

Yippie yi yo and seig heil!

Probably the most universally hated man of this century, dictator Adolf Hitler, founder of the Nazi Party in Germany, was enamored by the American Wild West when he was just a child. His favorite stories were by a German, Karl May, who, although he had never been to America, wrote dozens of novels about cowboys and Indians. Hitler taught himself how to throw a lasso and led his classmates in playing on these themes.

He probably also read the works of Heinrich Mollhousen, who has been called "the James Fennimore Cooper of Germany." Mollhousen had actually visited the American West and wrote frontier stories with authentic detail.

After Hitler became the chancellor of Germany, a $20,000 mortgage note was confiscated by the government. The note was secured by twenty sections of land near the town of Kit Carson, Colorado. The German family (possibly Jewish) who had the mortgage had inherited the note from an uncle who had been co-owner, with a Mr. Bauer, of most of the Kansas City stockyards.

Hitler ordered that the ranch property be put into his name as owner and demanded payment of the note. Bauer detested Hitler and refused the order. Instead, he relinquished 12,300 acres of land that he considered "worthless."

When war against Germany was declared on December 8, 1941, Hitler could no longer retain ownership to the property. The land reverted to the United States government's possession.

At the end of the war, a New Mexico senator arranged for the disposition of it. A man by the name of Jainway, from New Mexico, purchased the ranch. It has since been divided and sold several times. The name Adolf Hitler still remains on the abstract listings in Cheyenne County. ❖

The Bombing of Colorado in World War II

Japanese air attacks

In an attempt to demoralize the United States during World War II, the Japanese released more than 9,000 balloon-borne incendiary bombs, carried by the jet stream and designed to fall and explode on United States soil. Only about 300 of these actually reached North America, and those fell harmlessly, for the most part, on Pacific coastal regions. At least four, however, came inland as far as Western Colorado. There, unable to clear the mountains, they crashed and exploded near Delta, Collbran, and Pagosa Springs.

One of the explosions, near Robidoux Canyon in Delta County, was witnessed; the others were found only by their remains. The incidents were investigated but kept secret during the war years as a result of F.B.I. investigations. Michael Unsworth, of Michigan State University, has made a study of these bombs, verifying the sites of the explosions. The balloons were constructed of silk and paper.

Another "bombing" occurred in August of 1943 but was not the work of the Japanese, although the people of Grand Junction thought so at the time. A train hauling ammunition had something go wrong with its wheels as it sped westward through Debeque Canyon. When the locomotive reached that city, the car carrying the explosives was on fire and exploded in the railroad yards. The local newspaper proclaimed this was the first stateside city to be shelled in World War II. ❖

ABOUT
LAWS AND
OUTLAWS

A postman on "Norwegian snow shoes"

Those Postmen on Skis

Death-defying letter carriers

In the late 1870s and early 1880s, there were numerous mail carriers in Colorado who contracted to deliver mail to various isolated mountain towns. This job often involved using "Norwegian snow shoes" in the winter. These snow shoes were actually skis, sometimes as long as ten feet, which one balanced by the use of a long pole while navigating over the mountain terrain. The most famous of these Norwegian snow shoe mail carriers were the "Snowshoe Itinerant" John Dyer, a Methodist minister, who did the Fairplay-Leadville circuit and Albert Johnson, who crossed the range between Crystal and Crested Butte.

Retaining mail carriers was often a problem as well. The Postal Service headquarters in Denver seems to have had the most difficulty in keeping mail carriers for the San Juan mountains, noted for their frequent and devastating snowslides.

Swan Nilson, the carrier from Silverton to Ophir, was buried in a slide on December 23, 1883. Efforts to find his body proved fruitless. Then someone thought he had seen Nilson in a Leadville bar. Silverton residents were livid with anger, believing he had taken all their Christmas gifts and absconded with them. Two years later, though, his remains were found, and the people of Silverton were swept with guilt feelings for having suspected such a dastardly act from such a fine man. Postal officials in Denver kept his decomposed mail bag on display to remind other carriers of the heroic demands of their calling.

The town which seemed to have had the most trouble in mail delivery during the winter of 1879-80 was Rico. In January, the *Rico News* claimed that one Brewster, "a damned fraud," had contracted to carry mail to Silverton and had instead dumped the mail in an old cabin and deserted the run.

Later, the paper proclaimed in bold-faced type, "San Juan will yet send a delegation to hang or impeach fraudulent mail carriers."

A second mail disaster hit Rico the next month when the News reported that O.T. Tyler, a carrier bringing the mail from Parrot City (now La Plata on very detailed maps) had been frozen to death on the trail. Finally, a series of roads was established to improve the routes into Rico.

One of the most famous of the San Juan road builders was Otto Mears. He established mail routes, too. In 1875, he put into operation a system which was unique in the history of Colorado. This was mail carried by dogsled from Lake City to Silverton and Ouray.

For a time, this method worked well. When the snow became too deep and fluffy for even dogs, the service was stopped, much to the annoyance of recipients. Finally, Mears himself decided to deliver the mail on skis.

His only trip was in January of 1876. He spent three days getting from Lake City to Ouray and felt he was going to die from exhaustion. At one place, he had to slog through two feet of wet snow on a frozen river, with the water rushing below the ice. After that, he gave up on short-cuts through the mountains. ❖

These Were Some of the Laws

Civilians can't own white cars

When the mining camp of Empire, at the foot of Berthoud Pass, was established in 1860, it was called Valley City. While bothered by few laws, one ordinance did read, "No lawyer shall be permitted to practice" within the district. The penalty for violation was fifty lashes and banishment. Attorneys were banned from some other mining camps, too, including the town of Ruby, atop Kebler Pass near Crested Butte.

Murder was frowned upon in the Gregory Gulch gold diggings near what would become Central City and Blackhawk. The criminal code there stated: "Any person shooting ... another, except in self-defense, shall be fined $500 and receive as many stripes on his bare back as a jury of six may direct."

Among Denver laws, some of which remain on the books as of this writing, is one allowing the mayor to draft men of the city as needed for emergencies or law enforcement. This was first enacted as a precaution against Indian invasions.

Another Denver law required that a notice be posted on a park tree if an animal control officer had intentions of impounding any dog in the area. It was a violation of the law to drive cattle on Denver streets, and city employees were prohibited from having any debts. One still may not ride a horse in Denver over twenty miles per hour.

Still on the books is a highway department directive which requires an automobile driver to honk the horn when rounding the narrow defiles of any canyon.

White automobiles were banned to the general public at one time. In 1953, the State Revenue Department reminded owners that they were subject to fines of $1,000 and jail sentences of up to six months if found driving white cars. That privilege was reserved for Colorado State Patrol vehicles only. The writer has been unable to determine when this law was

repealed, but today white is highly recommended as the pre-
ferred "color" by safety experts and is very popular among
Colorado drivers.

It is still on the books that it is illegal to ride a horse while
intoxicated.

In Ouray the law required a stage coach driver to stop the
stage at least five miles from Ouray and let out anyone suspected of small pox or other contagious disease (would this
include a cold?). It was also illegal to transport the contents of
privies through town except between the hours of midnight
and 5 a.m. On the other hand, dead animals (including horses)
were to be removed within six hours of death.

Public morals were also of great concern in Ouray. It was
illegal for any woman to work as a waitress or bartender in
any saloon "for the purpose of attracting customers." Minors
could not frequent a billiard house, saloon, house of ill-repute
or bowling alley between 9 P.M. and 5 A.M. Presumably they
could legally be there at other times. ❖

Some Notes on Women's Suffrage in Colorado

Men crowded out the ladies at school elections

Susan B. Anthony, the famous women's suffragette, blamed "Mexicans in southern counties" of Colorado Territory for the defeat of the proposal in the 1877 election which would have given the women of Colorado the right to vote. In truth, the issue was defeated by such a large majority that the Mexican vote (which was mostly opposed) had very little effect on the results of the election.

Coloradans by and large wished to avoid any controversy relative to their recent promotion to statehood. It was apparently typical for the women's movement to blame minority ethnic groups for their defeat in other states before winning the national battle.

As a territory, Wyoming was the first political entity to grant universal women's suffrage. Colorado was the second and the first as a "state."

The ladies of Colorado did have a limited right to vote as early as 1880. Under the law at that time, women were allowed to cast their ballots but only in school elections. Apparently very few took advantage of this privilege. It seems that so many men jammed the polling places and dominated the process that women felt somewhat intimidated when trying to exercise their newly-found rights. ❖

Colorado's Cruelist Utopian Hoax

The Cotopaxi bubble

It is an oft-repeated story that Colorado was viewed as a favored locale for Utopian colonies in the early years. Most were failures in regard to their original socialistic purposes: Greeley, Longmont, Fort Amity and Deerfield, to name a few of the most famous. However, for pure exploitation of innocent farmers, the colony of Cotopaxi had to be the worst.

At a time when the Tsar of Russia was persecuting Jews with horrid "pogroms," refugees from farm villages came to the United States seeking a new life. There were available numerous regions for homesteading which would have fulfilled their dreams.

An unscrupulous Portuguese Jew named Emanuel Saltiel was able to deceive the Hebrew Immigrant Aid Society in New York with a nefarious scheme. That organization sent about fifty newly-arrived families out to a "farming Utopia" owned by Saltiel in Colorado, where they supposedly would be provided with homes, barns, and 160 acres of farmland each.

In 1882, the immigrants were loaned railroad fares to make the journey west and were to pay for that cost, in addition to payment for their assigned properties, out of earnings from their farms. Instead of buildings, they found only crude huts. Cotopaxi, on the Arkansas River between Canon City and Salida, is rocky canyon country with hardly a level space anywhere. There was no good farm land. Freezing temperatures destroyed most of their feeble efforts to grow any food on this thin soil. In order to survive, most of the men had to work in Saltiel's mines at near-starvation wages. When the settlers realized that they had been victimized by intent, rather than error, they left to work in Salida for the Denver and Rio Grande Railway as manual laborers.

Eventually, the Denver Jewish community heard of their plight and brought most of them to the city for re-settlement. At the end of three years, none were left in Cotopaxi. ❖

Whiskey Hole: An Early-Day Economic Welfare Program

Free mining for the unlucky

One of the most impressive gold discoveries in the so-called "Pike's Peak Gold Rush" of 1858 was at Tarryall on the edge of South Park. Prospectors who got there first rubbed their eyes in amazement. In the course of an old creek channel there were "scales of gold as big as watermelon seeds."

After this initial boom, though, it became more difficult to find the gold dust. Going upstream to find the mother lode, a few of the men were fortunate. Other newcomers were unable to find any pay dirt at all. There was one good source, however. It was called the Whiskey Hole.

Old vets of several months began to feel sorry for the newcomers. They set aside the Whiskey Hole as a place where only destitute prospectors could pan for their whiskey. Hundreds of men found enough dust to handle their accounts at the nearby saloon.

Eventually, there was so much claim-jumping going on in the Tarryall mining district that, when new finds were found on the other side of the mountain, most sourdoughs moved over there. It was decided at the outset in this camp that any infringement on another's claim would be dealt with in the most severe manner. Thus, they named the new camp Fairplay. ❖

When Baldwin Conquered Vulcan

Sullivan's siege

They are both ghost mining camps now. Baldwin was seventeen miles north of Gunnison and Vulcan was seventeen miles south of Gunnison. Each had a population of over two hundred on February 16, 1899, when the residents of Baldwin invaded Vulcan and captured the town.

It seems that a bully by the name of Steve Sullivan had been able to form his own union in Baldwin and proposed that Vulcan now be organized. Miners in the latter camp had run him out of town, suggesting that when and if they joined a union, it would be that of the Western Federation of Miners.

This rankled Sullivan, who got together a band of seventeen fellow workers, and on that cold winter day, they rode to Vulcan. First they cut the lone telephone line into Gunnison. Then they herded the women, children, and men who were not in the mine into the bunkhouse and forced them to sit on the floor under armed guard. The hoodlums then went house to house and confiscated all the weapons they could find.

When the bookkeeper for the mine tried to escape, he was brutally pistol-whipped. Guards were posted on the lone road leading into the town. The mine superintendent was forced to stand with his hands grasping an overhead beam in the bunkhouse prison. The victims were told that if any others tried to escape, they would all be "blown to pieces."

In spite of the warning, a blacksmith tried to sneak out the door. He was shot in the wrist and in the right lung. This did upset one of the invaders who had not counted on the necessity for this much violence. Conscience-stricken, he loaded the blacksmith on a wagon, hitched up a team, and set out for Gunnison with the injured man.

The raiders ordered the camp cook to prepare supper for all the people present. After eating, the invaders conducted another house search and took all the skis and snowshoes they found.

After a rudimentary breakfast the next morning, the miners were herded out to the one road leading from Vulcan. They were then ordered on a forced march to walk the eight miles at gunpoint to the railroad station at Iola (now submerged by Blue Mesa Lake). When one of the men complained, he was forced to remove his boots and continue the walk in his stocking feet.

At Iola, the men were kept standing in the frigid weather until the narrow-gauge train arrived. Despite attempts by the train crew to prevent boarding, the prisoners were forced to get on the train and told never to return. Of course, they got off at the next stop, Sapinero. By this time, as a result of the rescue of the injured man, Gunnison was aware of the incident so the gang returned to Baldwin.

A trial was held in Gunnison after the ring-leaders were arrested. However, the jury decided this whole incident was not criminal, merely a union dispute. Therefore, the case was dismissed. ❖

Dealing with Confirmed Criminals

Advocates of emasculation

In 1895, Dr. B.A. Arbogast, of Breckenridge, recommended that "all professional and confirmed criminals should, before they are liberated (from prison), undergo an operation that would effectively prevent their procreation."

He also advised, in *Transactions of the Colorado State Medical Society*, that "castration, with our antiseptic surgery and anesthesia, is painless and safe and would have a greater deterrent effect on the vicious than our penitentiaries and gallows." These views were cited in *Rocky Mountain Medicine*, a carefully researched book by Robert Shikes.

Emasculation was often recommended for crimes of rape or molestation. An armed mob in Montrose got out of hand on election night in 1904. They forced a Dr. Schermerhorn and a Dr. Coleman to go into the jail to perform an emasculation on one H.F. Allen. Allen had been accused of an attack on a small girl.

The captive doctors insisted that the prisoner must be taken to the hospital for the operation. As soon as he arrived, the accused man escaped and was never recaptured. ❖

The Honor System of the Wilderness

Don't lock that door!

As late as the 1940s, people who owned cabins in the isolated regions of the plains and mountains of Colorado felt a necessity to leave them unlocked and stocked with food. Some person traveling in the area in a storm might need access to such a sanctuary. On the other hand, the individual who took advantage of this opportunity was honor-bound to clean the cabin properly and to restock it when and if the chance later afforded itself. Some owners even kept rifles and ammunition in the cabins in case they were needed.

Another custom which was widely observed was the placing of a pair of skis or snowshoes at the trailhead in case they were needed to reach snow hikers or climbers in the winter. It was considered about the same as stealing a horse for anyone to remove or disturb such vital means of transportation in the back country.

Unfortunately, after World War II, there seemed to be many cases of theft and vandalism to the cabins. Owners reluctantly placed locks on the doors and shuttered the windows. One Texas owner of a cabin near Lake City in the 1950s, though, went a step further. As he left in the autumn, he rigged up a shotgun to fire at anyone entering the door. The last time he ever forgot anything was the next summer when he was the victim who opened the door. ❖

Colorado's Most Outrageous Mass Murderer

Graham's massacre in the air

On the evening of November 1, 1955, a United Airlines Mainliner DC6-B took off from Denver's Stapleton Field. It exploded in the sky near the town of Longmont, a few minutes later. All forty-four people aboard were killed instantly, murdered by John Gilbert Graham.

With painstaking research, authorities finally established the guilt. Graham, twenty-four, had wished to inherit the property and insurance proceeds of his mother, Mrs. Daisy King, fifty-four. In those days, insurance policy vending machines were common in major airports. This crime probably brought an end to the practice by which nervous travelers could make last-minute investments on their lives. Graham's prime mistake was to purchase one of these policies in his mother's name with himself as the beneficiary. He carelessly failed to notice that she was supposed to sign it.

John Gilbert Graham in custody

Of course, he did not want her to have any inkling that he had planted twenty-five sticks of dynamite with a timing device in her luggage. Apparently the ever-thoughtful son, he had driven her to the airport and checked the bags himself paying an overweight charge on one of the items.

A dropout from the University of Denver, Graham was Mrs. King's only heir, and the insurance policy he purchased would have netted him another $37,500.

Investigators traced the dynamite purchase to a Kremmling hardware store and the timing device to a Denver clockmaker.

Graham was executed in the gas chamber at the state prison in Canon City in January 1957. ❖

ABOUT SUPERLATIVE PLACES

Grand Lake, western terminal of the Adams Tunnel

The World Longest Water Tunnel

A blue diversion

Throughout the past century, there have been numerous diversions of water from Colorado's Western Slope to the eastern side of the state, where nine out of ten citizens of Colorado reside. Most of the early works were slight, even including the Moffat Tunnel, which may have been financed more for water than for railroad purposes.

Large-scale projects, though, began with the massive Colorado-Big Thompson Project, completed in 1952. Central to the project was the Adams Tunnel, 13.1 miles long. It was drilled beneath the Continental Divide between Grand Lake and Estes Park. This was a signal to start a rash of tunnels and siphons to water thirsty cities of the Front Range corridor.

At twenty-three miles in length, the Roberts Tunnel, between Dillon Lake and the South Platte Canyon, was billed as the longest water tunnel in the world at the time it was bored. It still holds that record. It was completed in 1963.

The Roberts Tunnel diverts water from the Western Slope's Blue and Snake Rivers into the Denver watershed. At one point, it is 4,465 feet below the surface of the Continental Divide.

Western states that depend on these waters have vehemently complained about those "thefts." Nevertheless, there are even new proposals to divert more water. As a matter of fact, every snowflake that falls on the Western Slope has already been over-appropriated. ❖

World's Highest Telescope in the 1880s

Putting Del Norte on the map

George Darley, a Presbyterian minister who built the first church on the Western Slope at Lake City, was also the founder of the short-lived Presbyterian College of the Southwest at Del Norte. Founded in 1885, the college had a continuous struggle for survival before closing down in 1906.

One of the most extraordinary features of the College of the Southwest, though, was a domed telescope observatory atop Mount Lookout at the edge of town. This was billed as the highest observatory in the world. Darley hoped it would draw sightseers from other nations as well as other states, putting Del Norte and his college on the map.

While trying to raise money in New York for the school, Darley dramatized his cause in a manner not exactly politically nor tastefully correct. He told of the recently-departed "war-whoop of savages" and pointed out that "On the west we are face to face with filthy Mormonism, on the south with hoary Romanism...both inexorable enemies" to his cause. This type of plea must have worked with his listeners, though, as he did get enough to finance the college and the observatory for a few years more. ❖

The Original Hard Rock Cafe

Empire deals with audacity

In 1971, with the advent of music known as "hard rock," a cafe in London, England, opened with the name of the Hard Rock Cafe. The establishment became so popular that today there are corporate branches of this cafe in most of the leading cities of the world and in many resorts.

However, as early as 1934, the Empire Cafe in the town of Empire, which is located at the foot of Berthoud Pass, changed its name to Hard Rock Cafe, honoring the hard rock miners of the area who often lodged in its upstairs rooms. While the ownership has changed over the years, the name has remained the same.

Several years ago, the international Hard Rock chain had such effrontery as to demand that this restaurant drop that name because of the chain's copyrighted moniker. However, Empire was there first, and the suit was thrown out of court.

As of this writing, it is still the Hard Rock Cafe and is favorably known for its food rather than loud music. Until recently under the proprietorship of Norm Duensing, the town of Empire, which owns the building, has agreed that the name will be permanent on that structure in the future.

There is one other Hard Rock Cafe, a later-named one in California, which also preceded the international chain, according to Mr. Duensing, and it, too, is void of the current music fad. ❖

Largest Letter in the Western Hemisphere

A student extracurricular project

The gigantic "W" on Tenderfoot Mountain overlooking Gunnison was listed as the largest man-made letter in the world by The *Guinness Book of World Records* until 1971. That was the year in which the word, READYMIX, was constructed on the ground near East Balldonia, West Australia. The letters were designed to be read from airplanes flying high overhead. At 600 feet in length,they are much larger than the "W."

The "W" emblem, designating Western State College, was laid out by students in 1921 and measures about 400 feet by 350 feet. On occasions such as Homecoming, the letter is lit by torches. There was once a plan to outline it with electric lights. This plan had to be abandoned when aeronautic officials were made aware of the scheme. The mountain is just above the Gunnison airport. This could be very confusing to some lost pilot flying over that area on a snowy night.

When it became the fashion to try to preserve scenery in its natural state, ecology-minded students decided it was time to remove the letter. On further consideration, though, they realized that it had been in place too long. To remove it would damage the mountain far more than the presence of the letter, as the uncovered soil would erode into gulches which would eventually become gullies. ❖

Dimes in the Black Canyon?

They never got to Phoenix

In about 1880, four wagons left the Denver Mint for Phoenix, Arizona. At least one of them was loaded with kegs of newly-minted dimes.

As the wagon train was traveling along the north rim of the Black Canyon of the Gunnison, it was possibly raided by Indians. In any event, it was never heard from again. Speculation runs that the men were killed, and the train was raided for the horses. The dimes, at least one keg, must have been thrown over the edge.

Chipeta, wife of Ouray

In 1973, a visitor to the canyon found three gallons of dimes in one of the draws as well as the remains of a very old keg. He was too old to go looking for more but he told his story to *Lost Treasure* magazine.

These uncirculated coins would have quite a value today. Well, that's the story, anyway. It seems that any inaccessible place has a treasure yarn to go with it.

As for the Black Canyon, there is another old story told around the region. This one proposes that when Ouray, the Ute leader, died just before the Utes were banished from the region, his widow, the famous Chipeta, was thoroughly disgusted with the whites. In a fit of anger, she took all the money which had been saved by a stipend from the federal government and threw it into the Black Canyon. Possible, but highly unlikely. ❖

Old Colorado City's Post Office Box

No mail for the legislators

The original Colorado City, now a part of Colorado Springs, does take rightful pride in the fact that it was, in 1861, the first territorial capital city of Colorado. It was also the designated county seat of El Paso County.

What fleeting glory it had! The legislators met there for only a few minutes, just long enough to adjourn to Denver. It seems there were no places for the first elected assembly to stay overnight.

When the railroad arrived, it bypassed the town of Colorado City, which, according to the founders of nearby Colorado Springs, had become almost a ghost town. However, the county clerk, Irving Holbert, still lived there and represented El Paso County in the territorial legislature.

With the establishment of Colorado Springs in 1871, whatever mail was sent to Colorado City was taken to the only remaining store in that town. There it was simply dumped into a soap box. Anyone living in Colorado City just sorted through the mail to take whatever was addressed to him or her.

The final outrage came in 1877, when County Clerk Holbert had to move to the new court house in Colorado Springs.

Today, though, that district of the city is proud to welcome tourists to numerous arts and crafts shops and to display the original cabin which was once the seat of Colorado government. ❖

The Twelve Thousand Keys of Baldpate

Including one for Buckingham Palace

Named for the novel, *The Seven Keys to Baldpate*, by Earl Derr Biggers, the historic Baldpate Inn stands beneath the awesome diamond east face of Long's Peak. In addition to other antique attractions, the collection of keys there is believed to be the world's largest, or at least nearly so. In 1988, the official key count was 12,107. Guests and other persons from all over the world have donated to the key collection.

Among the prizes of the display are keys to George Washington's headquarters building, Adolf Hitler's desk, Mozart's wine cellar, and the front door of "little Brown Church in the Vale."

Ironically the inn itself is believed to have no front door key. There are keys inside to Buckingham Palace and the Frankenstein Castle. Many odd and home-made keys are on display such as keys which were made out of spoons used in an escape from the Colorado State Penitentiary in 1896. ❖

America's First Junior High School

Tossed out as a bad idea

At the beginning of the twentieth century, most public education was divided into eight years of elementary school and four years of secondary school. However, one problem with the system was that too few students went on to high school after completing the eighth grade.

A remarkable Leadville superintendent of schools, Edward C. Elliot, decided in those days that if students could have an earlier taste of secondary education, they might stay in school through high school. He established what has been recognized as the first junior high school, comprised of the seventh and eighth grades.

However, he soon realized that this new school arrangement was no better than the earlier one in retaining students. As a result, he decided that high school should begin in the eighth grade.

Until 1954, Leadville had the unique arrangement which embraced a seven-five plan, with seven years of elementary and five years of high school. Eighth graders were known as "sub-freshmen."

Incidentally, this innovative educator went on to become president of Purdue University. ❖

A Hidden Retreat for Scientists

Gothic's biological think tank

About seven miles above the resort area of Crested Butte is the site of the old mining town of Gothic. This is now the location of the Rocky Mountain Biological Institute, where some of the nation's most respected biologists spend their summers in research, writing and relaxation.

The institute was founded by John C. Johnson, a biologist with Western State College in Gunnison. Originally located in the Taylor River Canyon, it was moved to Gothic after it had attracted the attention of other prominent scholars from such places as Yale and Stanford Universities. In Gothic, there is higher than normal rainfall for the mountain regions. This leads to a great variety of plant life, insects and birds. The region between there and Crested Butte has been called the wildflower capital of the state.

Individual scientists purchased and remodeled the old cabins of the village and built abodes consistent with the mining-town style. There, away from the demands of urban and pressurized academic worlds, they are free to write and pursue their interests undisturbed. Graduate students are occasionally allowed to carry out specific studies there, and the institute offers, at times, seminars to which the public is invited.

This region has many beautiful mountain trails. One leads to Judd's Falls, a spectacular cataract. There, a bench has been built for quiet contemplation. The bench is a memorial to Garwood Judd, a miner who doggedly remained in the otherwise deserted mining town until his death. He was known as "the man who stayed." ❖

Did "No Night in Creede" Mean Something Else?

Was it merely light bulbs?

One of the most famous couplets about any mining town has been that of Cy Warman who, as editor of the *Creede Chronicle* over a century ago, wrote: "It's day all day in the daytime, And there is no night in Creede."

This line has usually been considered descriptive of booming mining camps in the Rockies, where saloons, casinos, and other enterprises remained open around the clock to furnish rollicking excitement; where men on day and night shifts traded sleeping quarters and roamed around town at all hours.

Between upper and lower Creede

However, in the *Rocky Mountain Almanac* for 1989, editor Lee Olson pointed out that this poem came out the same week that Creede had installed electric lights throughout the town. It even referred to itself as the "electric city."

That would have been in March of 1892, not long after Telluride's L.L. Nunn proved the efficacy of alternate current, making that town the first electrified community in the world.

This suggests a totally new meaning to Warman's lines. Could it be that he was merely celebrating the fact that the entire community was enjoying brightness all night long? While not as dramatic as the earlier interpretation, the lines just may have been misunderstood. ❖

ABOUT

COLORADO

CLIMATE

The snow angel of Mt. Shavano

The Angel of Shavano and the Holy Cross

A frozen goddess overlooks Salida

One of the interesting symbolic snow forms in Colorado is the "Angel of Shavano," which usually appears above Salida in June. It is a spectacular form of a great angel on 14,229-foot Shavano Peak and usually lasts only a few days. The snow fields are the remnants of the winter cover which still fill the deep gullies above timberline.

Various legends abound. One claims it was never seen until it appeared following the settlement of a major labor dispute in the area. With the propensity the pioneers had for making up Indian legends, there is one which holds that Ute "Chief" Shavano converted to Christianity and that the angel has appeared on his namesake peak ever since. For those who prefer Roman mythology, Jupiter changed a goddess into ice and put her there until she could save the valley below from tragedy. When there was a major drought in the area below, she melted and gave water to save the people of that region. What was Jupiter messing around in the Rockies for, anyway?

Of course the most famous of these snow-filled formations was that of the Mount of the Holy Cross, at the other end of the Sawatch Range from Shavano. It towers above the town of Minturn. This formation became a source of Christian veneration from the earliest explorations until World War II. At some time during the war, debris filled an arm of the cross and ruined the effect. What had once been an official national monument lost its rating. People who had once gathered at Shrine Pass, above Redcliff, to view the miraculous sight, stopped coming.

Some saw deep symbolism in the geological phenomenon, claiming the nation had become sinful. A few Leadville people said that military trainees at the Tenth Mountain Division's Camp Hale had used it as a target and destroyed the cross. This latter myth is virtually an impossibility, considering the short-range artillery used by the Army mountaineers. ❖

How Deep Was That Snow?

Only the chimneys could be seen

Colorado's greatest recorded snow depth occurred back in 1899 at the town of Ruby, a few miles above Crested Butte, near the top of Kebler Pass. That one storm piled up 254 inches and buried the buildings in many places so that only the stove pipes coming out of the miners' shacks could be seen. That same storm buried a narrow-gauge train between Leadville and Fremont Pass. Skiers from Leadville went up and dug out the chilled and frightened passengers and crew.

As to ski area depths, the largest amount of total snow in a season is that recorded at Wolf Creek Pass, on the southern edge of the state. There, the average snowfall is between 500 and 600 inches during the winter.

Denver itself has had some classic snowstorms. The record for that city was thirty-three inches which came down in one onslaught in December of 1913. That's when some of the first skiing took place within the metropolis, as experienced instructors gave free lessons on the capitol grounds.

Actually, there is a very wide range in snowfall throughout the state. Delta, for instance, has less total precipitation on the average than does Tucson, Arizona! The total amount of rain and snow moisture content measures only 7.7 inches per year while Tucson gets about 10.6 inches. ❖

Gunnison Basks in Frozen Sunshine

Free meals on cloudy days

The town of Gunnison has garnered the dubious honor of having the lowest average temperatures of any city in the contiguous 48 states. Nevertheless, the locals are quick to point out that it just doesn't seem that cold because of the rarity of winter wind and the abundance of sunny days. Skiers often go out to the slopes of nearby Crested Butte in temperatures of 30 to 40 degrees below zero Fahrenheit. The famous La Veta Hotel used to offer a free meal on any day the sun did not shine. The sun did not shine only sixteen days in the sixty years during which the offer stood. ❖

Cattlemen's Day in Gunnison

When It Snowed Ducks on I-70

They crashed at the Eisenhower Tunnel

It was a dark night in the fall of 1977 when Colorado State Trooper Gary Eshelman was driving up the western approach to the Eisenhower Tunnel on Interstate 70. The snow was falling heavily before his headlights. As there was almost no other traffic, it seemed surprising to him when he saw something fluttering onto the road.

Stopping to examine, Gary was amazed to see that it was a duck, killed when it struck the hard road surface. Before he could go further, there were other ducks falling from the sky! Some landed in the soft snow to the side of the highway and were still alive. The trooper picked up one and saw that its wings were coated with ice. He put it into the patrol car, where it revived and began to quack. In the meantime, ducks continued to fall all around him.

Eshelman radioed to the Denver central control center, saying, "You've heard of it raining cats and dogs? Well, up here it's snowing ducks!" The dispatcher would not believe him at first, but he knew no one could imitate the sounds coming from the disgruntled fowl in the car.

Continuing on through the tunnel, Gary found the same thing was happening on the east approach. He talked to the tunnel night engineer who supplied him with some huge four-foot by four-foot cardboard cartons in which some equipment had been shipped.

In the ensuing hours, the trooper picked up thirty-two living ducks, of whom twenty-six eventually survived. When they were released the next morning, the ducks just walked around in a daze. It was late in the day before they felt up to trying their wings to continue what was apparently a southward migration. ❖

Colorado's Worst Dust Storm

When the wildfowl suffocated

During the days of the Dust Bowl in the 1930s, some of the massive dust storms that blew across the eastern plains of Colorado were so dense that they actually blocked out the sunshine and caused wide-spread panic among animals, not to mention some very major discouragement for farmers and ranchers. Possibly the worst of these dust storms occurred on April 14, 1935.

On that day a wall of dust a thousand feet high and more than 200 miles in width swept through the region from the north and then into Kansas to the east, traveling at an estimated sixty miles per hour. The density of the storm was such that it was said to have suffocated entire flocks of geese and ducks.

In an attempt to try to preserve farmland, the government and Colorado farmers planted thousands of quick-growing Chinese Elms and Russian Olives along the edges of the fields. The elms today are held in great disdain but they did come to the rescue back in those days when they effectively cut the impact of the dust storms. ❖

The Magic Crossing of a Flooded River

They didn't even get wet feet

There have been some horrendous stories of the spring meltdown of heavy mountain snowpacks and the often disastrous floods that result.

One of the most difficult stories to believe was substantiated by a number of eyewitnesses and apparently really occurred in 1906.

A herd of cattle was being driven to summer range through the town of Paonia, located on the North Fork of the Gunnison River, which was then at flood stage. The route of the cattle drive required that the river must be crossed. When the men and cattle drive reached Paonia in the evening, however, the flood was at full crest.

The cowboys decided it would be better to stay over and attempt the crossing the next morning, when they hoped the cool night would reduce the level of the flood.

However, when they rode out the next morning, they found the cattle grazing on the other side of the river! No, they hadn't swum the river at night. During the night, the river had changed course, cutting behind the herd! ❖

Of Droughts and Super-Droughts

A major exception to the cycles

According to dendrochronologists, those who study tree rings for evidence of climate changes, Colorado seems to be subject to severe and sustained droughts about every thirty-five to forty years. Somehow, this is also coincidental with sun spot activity according to astronomers. The limited history of the so-called White Man in Colorado also bears out this record.

During the gold-rush days of 1858-59, settlers were told by the native Indians not to build too close to the banks of Cherry Creek and the South Platte River in the area that was to become present-day Denver. There was a drought period at that time. In their arrogant feeling of greater intelligence, the newcomers defied the advice and were totally wiped out in the first of the severe floods in those basins, which occurred in 1864. (Denver has taken a long time to learn not to build on its flood plains and that reservoirs only hold a limited amount of water.)

The next major drought period occurred in the 1890s at a time when the repeal of the Silver Purchase Act had devastated most of Colorado's mining economy, too. Then, in the 1930s, during the Great Depression, there was still another severe drought.

This would indicate another drought in the late 1970s, and by this time scientists and historians were expecting it. The new ski industry, however, apparently either didn't know or didn't care about such cycles. Many millions of dollars went into loans based upon an unrealistic estimate of minimum ski days for both the slopes and the related businesses. The drought arrived just about on schedule and hit these regions in such a way that when skiers flew in at Christmas, they found only grass at the foot of the slopes in some ski areas. Since then, most major ski resorts have installed snow-making equipment.

The record drought that can be verified was recorded only in the tree rings of ancient growth. In the latter part of the thirteenth century, a drought which lasted twenty-four years was one of the most apparent causes for the evacuation of the Anasazi culture from such places as Mesa Verde, where they had dwelt for 1200 years or more. One of the most sobering thoughts modern day futurists can conceive is that if it happened once, it could happen again. Imagine what a quarter-century drought could do to the entire southwestern portion of the United States today! With every snowflake over-appropriated to places from Denver to Los Angeles, the lack of water would result in almost total devastation of the economy as it now exists. ❖

ABOUT
FLORA AND
FAUNA

From Frank Leslie's Illustrated Newspaper

Grizzly Legends

And Moccasin Bill's dilemma

When it comes to tales told of grizzly bears anywhere in the West, one story is usually beaten by another even more fantastic tale. While it is believed that the grizzly probably is extinct in Colorado as of this writing (one was killed in the San Luis Valley as late as the 1970s), memories abound with encounters between those great creatures and mankind.

As for the most famous, "Old Mose," as he was called, was supposed to have slaughtered twenty men, a thousand deer, and hundreds of cattle before Jim Anthony finally cornered him and killed him in 1904. It's true that Jim killed him, all right, and his estimated weight in the autumn months would have been over 1,200 pounds. However, a recent study of that legend by Jim Perkins shatters some of the other myths about this critter.

Perkins researched the stories of that master of murder in the Black Mountain area of South Park. While many ranchers and hunters reported seeing Mose on the prowl, he probably never did kill a man and may only have been responsible for the murder of two Hereford bulls. That Old Mose was big, though, cannot be refuted. His hide measured ten feet from nose to tail, and his front paws were eight inches in width. It is believed he was about twelve years old when he met his doom.

While that story has not been completely squelched, there is room for another bear legend contender to take over as the most remarkable in Colorado.

Up in the West Elk Mountains near Crawford, they tell the story of "Moccasin Bill" Perkins, who was quite a hunter in that region at the beginning of the twentieth century. It seems that Bill was out with his special type of gun, a double-barreled affair with one bore for rifle bullets and the other for shot, when he encountered a grizzly cub, which, carelessly, he shot with the rifle bore. When the mother of the cub jumped out at him in a murderous frenzy, he scrambled up a small willow tree, with the snarling teeth of the enraged bear nipping at his heels. Having shot his only rifle bullet, Bill had only the shot bore left.

As the huge monster opened her mouth to chomp off his foot, the hunter stuck the shotgun down her gullet and fired. Sick with her innards full of buckshot, she dropped from the scrubby tree and wandered off into the woods to die. That may be the only case in history of a grizzly bear being killed with a single load from a shotgun. ❖

The Busiest of Beavers

A ninety-foot-high dam

According to the best judgement of geologists, Rifle Falls, which is just north of the town of Rifle, flow over what was once a beaver dam of between 90 and 100 feet in height. This dam must have been built by the mother of all beavers, as it gradually turned to limestone with the action of the calcified water which it impounded. The startling aspect, though, is the enormous size. If a beaver dam gets as high as 10 feet above the stream bed, it's considered mighty high these days.

Actually, Colorado almost ran out of beaver in the nineteenth century due to the demand for beaver hats. When Japan was opened to trade in 1853, the style switched to silk toppers, although Europe and the eastern part of North America had already been trapped clean of beaver. Even Colorado was running a bit short. Some additional beaver were brought down from Wyoming. Now, with most of their natural predators gone, there is a serious overpopulation of the crafty rodents. ❖

This Tree Was Alive When Socrates Taught

Volcanic ash at South Park in 1815

According to the U.S. Geological Survey, the oldest tree in Colorado is located above the town of Fairplay. It is a bristlecone pine which is well over 2,400 years of age. It was found by researcher Craig Brunstein in 1990. While still alive, it shows its age, with only a few small branches of live needles stemming from bark which is now sixteen inches thick.

It had its beginnings at a time when the Athenians lost the Peloponnesian War to the Spartans and the Hanging Gardens of Babylon were still growing. Its tree rings have revealed droughts and cold spells through the ages, giving scientists knowledge of long-time climate patterns in the mountains of central Colorado. As an example, the tree rings indicate a record cold spell around 1815, when volcanic ash in the atmosphere around the world kept the snow falling even in summer above South Park.

The exact location of the tree is being kept secret so that it will not be vandalized. ❖

Not So Old, But Mighty Big

Where Chipeta sat in council

Colorado's largest cottonwood, and there are a number of impressive ones, grows near the site of Old Pella, south of the town of Hygiene, in Boulder County. The tree's diameter is 105 inches at the base of the trunk, but its age is unknown, as experts fear taking a tree ring core would kill it. While there are those who believe it to be the largest of all plains cottonwoods, it seems the record is still held by one in Tama County, Iowa, which measured 130 inches and was still growing in 1984. To view this Colorado champion, check the map in Perry Eberhart's book, *Ghosts of the Colorado Plains.*

The largest blue spruce tree in the world grew near West Elk Creek in the Gunnison National Forest, north of Blue Mesa Lake. Towering 123 feet, it had a diameter of five feet three inches at the base of the trunk. It was first spotted by forest ranger James A. Lees in 1964 but was destroyed by lightning in 1995.

A landmark tree is the cottonwood growing at Delta, known as the Ute Council Tree. It is about 188 years old and barely clinging to life. It was here that the Utes met to hold some of their councils. This was verified by Chipeta, the widow of Ute leader Ouray. She is believed to have been the only Ute woman allowed to sit in council. The Council Tree is about 85 feet tall and has a trunk diameter of seven feet. ❖

Wildflowers, Tiny and Mammoth

Some not visible to the naked eye

The wildflowers of Colorado are of an amazing variety. In the short summer season the area above timberline is a wonderland of tiny blooms, replete with tiny blossoms which require the most close-up inspection even to be noticed. In late July, a person can bend down close to the tundra and find a variety of twenty or more different blossoms, flowers that are not even noticed while walking. Each has to be brightly colored in order to attract insects yet so small that it is not visible unless viewed from very close range.

The tiniest flowers in the state are not even visible to the naked eye. These include the blooms of the elm, ash or maple trees and bushes, which require a microscope or at least a magnifying glass for observation. For the casual observer, the smallest visible flower seems to be the arctic pearlwort (sagina saginoides). It has white petals only 1.3 to 3 millimeters in width and grows in the moist grasslands atop a stem no thicker than a thread. It is a very miniature relative of the carnation.

Probably the largest wildflower blossom which grows in Colorado is the mules-ear (wyethia amplexicaulis) which grows up to five inches in diameter. In truth, it is not a single blossom but appears as such to the observer. This is really a composite of many tiny individual flowers.

As for both wildflowers and cultivated blossoms, the impression that they are brighter in color at higher altitudes is not usually incorrect. Because of the shorter growing seasons, only the brightest are able to attract first attention of the pollinating insects and thus repropagate themselves. Towns high in the mountains have made much of their summer flower shows, with some having the most beautiful gardens found anywhere in the west. ❖

That's a Lot of Bull Elk!

The giant of dark canyon

Joe Plute, a Crested Butte hunter, was out looking for game to feed his family during the fall of 1899. He was down in a dark canyon, along Anthracite Creek, which runs west from Kebler Pass. He took aim at a massive bull elk and brought the huge animal down, taking home enough meat for the entire winter. He also kept the rack, which had a spread of 52 inches at the widest point. He never knew that he had bagged the largest elk rack in history.

It was not until 1961 that the Boone and Crockett Club, the keeper of such records, declared that rack the champion. It is on display at the visitor center in Crested Butte, something of a community heirloom and highly coveted by members of the community.

The second largest wapiti rack in Colorado was harvested by Robert G. Young in Summit County. The third largest was taken near Electric Mountain, about 12 miles southeast of Paonia. It was shot by John Burritt of Delta County in 1970. Burritt was already well known as an expert marksman, having been a member of the U.S. Biathlon team in the 1960 Winter Olympics. ❖

Ants Eat Bed Bugs

But do the ants stay in the bed?

A couple of generations ago, a popular go-to-bed rhyme ran: "Good night, sleep tight, and don't let the bed bugs bite!" For most people living in urban areas, it was merely a sort of joke, but bed bugs were very real in some of the isolated cabins of Colorado.

A wingless, bloodsucking insect, the bed bug (cimex lectularius) reproduced en masse during times when the cabins may not have been occupied. In an effort to fight the pests, ranchers would leave the beds in their cow camps doused with kerosene in the autumn, only to return in the summer to find the bedding infested with the fierce little pests.

Many remedies and precautions were tried such as having all four bed posts standing in dishes of kerosene, but the bugs seemed to reach the ceiling and then drop into the bedding. They also seemed impossible to get rid of. One gentleman's mother may have found the best solution of all.

In about 1900, Ernest Gear was a small child whose parents had homesteaded near Elbert, Colorado. There they had built a log cabin, which Ernest recalled was oozing with pitch. Even so, the sticky sap did not stop the bed bugs, who found a home in the cabin and forced a regular ritual of soaking all the bedding in kerosene. However, the bedsteads themselves housed the nasty critters.

Ernest remembered that there were some huge ant hills nearby and that his mother would kick over the colonies to enrage the inhabitants. She then put the bedsteads on top of the wrecked ant hills. In his autobiography, Gear recalled, "The ants would swarm over the beds and carry away the bugs, even going into the crevasses for the nits." ❖

Our Elusive State Bird

And his student cheering section

It may be safe to say that 95 percent of Coloradans have never seen nor heard the lark bunting, the official state bird of Colorado. Not a lark, nor a year-round resident, the bird thrives in the warm months on the lightly-populated grasslands of the eastern Colorado plains.

Lark Bunting

However those who are lucky or diligent enough to catch a glimpse of this distinguished flyer, or even more likely to hear it's beautiful call, have good reason to celebrate the cheerful visitor. It is quite common on the grasslands, away from towns. One place where it is seen most frequently is in the Pawnee National Grassland, northeast of Greeley.

The lark bunting, which is actually a finch, was the subject of a knock-down-drag-out debate in the State Assembly in 1931. Roy Langdon, a professor at the Colorado A. & M. College in Fort Collins, gave an eloquent speech in which he recommended the lark bunting for the distinction as state bird. Packing the galleries were 121 students from Fort Collins High School who came to enthusiastically endorse the motion. Somewhat opposed was State School Superintendent Katherine L. Craig who felt that some more widely-distributed bird would be a better selection.

Alas, other states had already claimed the bluebird and the meadowlark. Reporters covering the issue facetiously nominated the dodo or, perhaps, they remarked, the stool pigeon would be a possibility. More serious nominations were the snowy owl, the swallow, and the night owl.

After realizing that there was no cheering section for any other bird, the opponents who agreed with Miss Craig conceded, and the Assembly voted unanimously for the lark bunting. Long and proudly may he fly! ❖

ABOUT

ROCKS, MINERALS

AND MINES

SWEET SKIN

SWEET SKIN, a mythical Indian Maiden from the tribe of the
Utes, aspired to rival Hygia in health and beauty. In order to obtain
these priceless gifts Chief Ouray consulted with the Great Spirit and
advised SWEET SKIN to go and bathe in the steaming waters coming from the mountain side where the Mountain Sheep and the Elk
meet to feed and drink.

ANALYSIS

	Parts per Mil.		Parts per Mil.
SiO_2, Silica	50.2	Ca, Calcium	422.1
SO_4, Sulphate	1028.2	Mg, Magnesium	6.3
HCO_3, Bicarbonate	150	K, Potassium	10.9
CO_3, Carbonate	None	Na, Sodium	114.3
PO_4, Phosphate		Li, Lithium	None
H_2S, Hydrogen Sulphide	None	Oxygen to form SiO_3	13.3
Cl, Chloride	49	Oxygen Consuming	
Fe, Iron		Capacity	0.71
Al, Aluminum		As, Arsenic	
Fe_2O_3 } Iron and		Sr, Strontium	
Al_2O_3 } Aluminum Oxide.	3.5	Excess Carbon Dioxide	54.1
Mn, Manganese		Evaporation Solids	1818

The natural antiseptic quality of these Hot Springs is so great
that they might well be called healing waters and are very effective
in the treatment of Scrofula, Eczema, Skin Eruptions, Intestinal
Ulcers, Rheumatism and Kidney Poisons. Coming from the Vapor
Cave Sweats one notices that delicious fragrance of "Sweet Skin"
body odor natural to healthy childhood and free from the Uric Acid
or Kidney smell so common in age and infirmity.

The power of these waters to eliminate body poisons is so great
that inveterate tobacco users taking a course of baths often find
tobacco again tasting badly and to continue its use a nervous shock
almost like commencing its use again.

We invite you to use these waters to cleanse your system so that
good health may again give you happiness and the joy of living.
Rates, including room, meals and bath, $4.00 per day or $25.00 per
week. Park and camp privileges for auto tourists.

For Health, Rejuvenation, Recreation and Pleasure, visit the

"Sweet Skin" Radio-Active Hot Springs and Vapor Cave Baths

at OURAY, COLORADO

The most scenic city
in all the world

On D. and R. G. W. R. R. and Chief Ouray Highway

*The back of an advertisement for "Sweet Skin" lists
the minerals contained in the "curative" waters,
while the front of the card, at right, shows the building in
the scenic mountain town of Ouray.*

When Super-Radiation Was Thought Healthful

Soaking up the rays

Prior to the days of atomic energy, it was believed by many that if a little radiation could cure certain illnesses, a lot would lead to total health. All over the West, people flocked to sources of radioactivity in hopes of curing kidney stones, goiter, bronchitis, asthma, ulcers, gonorrhea and rheumatism.

Colorado's hot spring pools which had traces of radium were in demand, as were old mines with uranium elements. At Idaho Springs, one abandoned mine was a popular place in the mountains

where people would pay money for permission to sit for hours in "hot spots" furnished with benches. The hot springs pool at the town of Ouray advertised that it was "the most radioactive in the world." While the claims were not always published, there were some devotees of radiation who maintained that they had been cured of cancer.

Many people bought flasks of radium water to take home with them and attributed miraculous cures to the fluid. Advertisements nationwide promoted the wonderful healing properties of the resort spas and caves. Later, however, when the value of radiation was questioned, the state put an end to doubtful claims made by the promoters.

With the realization that radiation can be deadly, that aspect of Colorado's health industry died a sudden death. ❖

That Lovely Lapis Lazuli

Colorado's little-known gemstone

Most jewelers whom the writer has asked in Colorado have maintained that the source of the beautiful gemstone, lapis lazuli, is to be found only in Afghanistan. However, there are a few who are aware that one of the largest finds of this stone anywhere is on Italian Mountain in Gunnison County, Colorado.

The history of this blue mineral includes world-wide admiration. Some of the most elaborate screens produced in the Chang Dynasty of China included lapis. Lapis also appeared in hundreds of the lavishly inset marble panels of the Taj Mahal in India. Its deep blue was sought for the crowns of emperors. In crushed form, this stone made pigment for some of the most famous paintings of the Middle Ages and the Renaissance. It was believed by the ancients that powdered lapis lazuli would cure snakebites. Some of these gems are flecked with gold, iron pyrite (fool's gold) or calcite. Today, it is a very popular gem for use in both rings and necklaces.

None of the Colorado stones are pure, deep blue; they tend toward a more delicate tint. There is only limited quarrying of these stunning stones in Colorado. Apparently, Afghanistan can afford to produce them at a lower cost. ❖

Aquamarine and Pure Crystal

The hue of the ocean at 14,000 feet

Colorado's official gemstone is the aquamarine, a beautiful jewel named for the color of the ocean. It is not easy to find this stone. One must go to the 14,000 feet level of Mount Antero, between Salida and Buena Vista, in the Sawatch Range. Some specimens from this site have been included in museums around the world.

From that lofty gem locality, also, very pure quartz crystals have been discovered. A clear ball of crystal from there, measuring five and one-half inches in diameter, was exhibited at Chicago's World Columbian Exhibition in 1893. Legend related to this crystal ball made its remarkable size unique as no one at that time had found a rock crystal large enough to make a ball that size. Colorado gem expert Richard Pearl noted that this may be the same crystal ball which is on exhibit at the Chicago Museum of Natural History.

Lore has almost always included fantastic claims for pure crystal and mystic crystal balls, even from ancient times. Today thousands of people are ready to swear that wearing a quartz crystal on one's person will bring health and good fortune. ❖

Panning for gold

Record Nuggets

And a building of petrified wood

"Tom's Baby," a single gold nugget which weighed in at 135 ounces, was found by Tom Broves and Harry Lytton at Farcomb Hill near Breckenridge on July 23, 1887. Over more than a century of exhibition and perhaps some shaving, honest or dishonest, has reduced the nugget, broken and worn, to only 103 ounces. Nevertheless, it still outranks any other gold nugget found in Colorado.

Nugget forms of gold were not common in this state as they seem to have been in California or Alaska. More often, Colorado's gold usually appears as 'telluride,' in combination with other ores. "Tom's Baby" has been preserved in the stunning mineralogical exhibit at the Denver Museum of Natural History.

The North American record was held by an Aspen mine for the largest silver nugget found back in 1894. While it has since disappeared, the specimen weighed 1,840 pounds, and contained a silver content of slightly over 93 percent pure sterling.

While petrified wood is abundant in several areas of Colorado, one of the most interesting uses of the colorful stone may be found in Lamar. In 1932, W.G. Brown built a service station out of the collector-quality material, partly as a tourist attraction. It was once featured in Robert Ripley's syndicated cartoon panel, "Believe It or Not!" ❖

Ho, Hum — Just Silver and Gold

When no one seemed to care

One of the historical mysteries about Colorado's mineral wealth is that the Spanish, who established Santa Fe in 1609, did not discover and develop the gold and silver in what is now Colorado. Almost the entire quest of that empire had been based on the value of gold in the New World. It had made Spain the wealthiest nation of Europe. Did not these conquistadores penetrate the regions of the north in such a search? There is little or no evidence of any organized expeditions for that purpose.

If they didn't care, neither did the Americans, at least for a long time. When Zebulon Pike met one James Purcell in Santa Fe in 1807, Purcell told him about gold in the northern ranges. Pike duly included that in his report but it created no special excitement. Adventurer Anthony G. Bettay wrote to Thomas Jefferson in 1808 to report that he had found silver on a tributary of the South Platte River. Historian Charles J. Bayard of Colorado State University deduced that it may have been in what later became the Georgetown and Silver Plume districts. Jefferson replied only that such a discovery was "interesting."

Coming even before the fur trade, it must have been that these discoveries were offset by the hazards of crossing the Great Plains, discouraging even the greediest of adventurers. Probably the California gold rush of 1849 was what inflamed the lust leading to the Colorado excitement a decade later. ❖

Grand Junction Booms: Uranium and Tailings

Those fickle federal fiats

One of the biggest mineral booms in Colorado history resulted from the demand for raw materials to produce nuclear power in the 1950s. The center of the search for radioactive minerals in this state and Utah was Grand Junction, where the Atomic Energy Commission (AEC) established its raw materials purchasing depot.

That city was also the site of the most extensive refining operations, in which the pure material would be extracted from the raw ore. This left huge piles of debris, much of which was then used in landscaping and construction within the city. In 1959, when the Colorado Department of Public Health raised questions regarding this practice, the federal officials were scornful, pointing out that there was no more danger in the tailings than would be found in one's watch dial. It was generally considered unpatriotic in Grand Junction to criticize the AEC, which had brought so much growth and wealth to western Colorado.

Eventually, however, the AEC was abolished. In the 1970s a new agency, the Nuclear Regulatory Commission, was in charge of the radioactive material policies. It, with the enthusiastic support of the new Environmental Protection Agency, declared that all of the tailings must be removed as they were dangerous to the health and well-being of the local populace. Many experts familiar with the processes involved were startled to learn that some tailings sites could be considered that dangerous.

If there had been earlier underestimation of the remaining radioactivity in the tailings, there were now charges of overestimation. A person would have to live in the same house for forty years and eat the dirt in the back yard to get enough radiation to injure health, according to some respected estimates. In the meantime, publicity was such as to portray the city as an entity glowing in the dark, so little was known about the properties of the tailings.

However, Uncle Sam came to the rescue, offering to pay the cost of digging up all the tailings and transporting them to a safer place out on the desert. This involved the construction of a new nine-mile paved highway for trucks to haul the material and a railroad contract for transportation for a part of the distance. In addition, it included millions of dollars to employ people to remove the tailings. All of this came to pass at a time when Grand Junction had been hit with another dismal bust, the abandonment of oil shale production.

Almost at once, it was unpatriotic to criticize the tailings removal project. The city got a new swimming pool to replace one which had been landscaped with residue, and there were a multiplicity of other earth-moving projects throughout the urban area. When the project was completed, Grand Junction had realized far more income from the removal of the waste than it ever had from the initial boom that created the problem. ❖

Minerals Named After Coloradans

Immortalized in the stones

Back in 1941, Richard M. Pearl, then secretary-treasurer of the Colorado Mineral Society, compiled a list of minerals named for Colorado people. Usually, the custom was to name the mineral after its discoverer, although that was not always the rule. Following are those immortalized in the names of minerals:

Cahnite was named for Lazard Cahn of Colorado Springs.

Pearceite, for Dr. Richard Pearce of Denver.

Hillebrandite, for Dr. W.F. Hillebrand of Denver.

Warrenite, for E.R. Warren of Crested Butte.

Emmonsite, after Samuel F. Emmons of Denver.

Rickardite, after T.A. Rickard of Gunnison.

Schiermerite, for J.F.L. Schiermer of Idaho Springs.

Beegerite, honoring Hermann Beeger of Denver.

Weissite, honoring Dr. Louis Weiss of Gunnison.

Tysonite, for S.T. Tyson of Colorado Springs.

Ilesite, after Dr. Malvern W. Iles of Leadville.

Kentsmithite, memorializing J. Kent Smith of Paradox.

Crossite, for Whitman Cross of Denver.

Rilandite, after J.L. Riland of Meeker.

Nicholsonite, for another Leadville man, S.D. Nicholson.

Vandiestite, honoring Peter H. Van Diest of San Luis.

Overite, for Colorado Springs' Edwin Over, and lastly,

Doughtyite, for G. Doughty of Austin. ❖

Boredom With an Eight-Hour Workday

The perils of leisure

John C. Osgood, one-time owner of the Colorado Fuel and Iron Corporation, has been rightly celebrated as an enlightened capitalist in the era of the "Robber Barons." For the miners of coal on the Crystal River, he built what is considered to be the model mining town, Redstone. It is still a beautiful village.

When the labor disputes were rife in Colorado, at the beginning of the twentieth century, one of the issues was the demand by unions for an eight-hour workday. Osgood addressed the Colorado State Assembly, saying that such an idea was preposterous. He pondered over what miners might do with their time if they worked only eight hours and slept for only eight hours. It would be an invitation to boredom and would lead to moral degeneration!

The inevitable limitations were established in spite of his plea. Osgood adjusted by providing the workers in Redstone with a fine recreation center, library, and a guest hotel.

Unfortunately, such powers as the Rockefellers and the Goulds became too much of a challenge for the kindly Osgood when they set their hooks for the Colorado Fuel and Iron Corporation. The New York capitalists wrestled control of the steel plant and its coal mines from him. From that time on, labor relations deteriorated, reaching their lowest point in the so-called Ludlow Massacre in southern Colorado. ❖

ABOUT NAMES AND PLACES

Mount Sneffels, located in Ouray County, Colorado

It Was Certain To Happen

A runny nose in the San Juans

Among the highest peaks in the San Juan range, overlooking the towns of Ouray and Ridgway, is the towering and spectacular Mount Sneffels. Many visitors to the area are curious as to how the peak got its strange-sounding name.

In 1874, the region was first mapped by what became known as the Hayden Survey. In the process, many of the members of the party climbed the dominant 14,150 foot peak. Geologist Fredrick Endlich was among one of the first groups to reach the top. He had been reading an 1864 novel, *Journey to the Center of the Earth*, by the famous French storyteller Jules Verne.

As Endlich gazed down upon the Blue Lakes Basin below the summit, he was reminded of the great crater described in the novel. The peak in the novel was a fictional Icelandic mountain named Snaefellsjokull. Asked to suggest a name for the mountain, he first suggested Snaifellsjokull, but his comrades decided the name was too cumbersome. It was finally agreed to call the peak Mount Sneffels.

That peak is probably the most photographed peak in Colorado with only the possible exception of the Maroon Bells near Aspen. Mount Sneffels has appeared on hundreds of calendars, in thousands of articles, and in dozens of "coffee-table books."

As was certain to happen, though, people had difficulty with the name. It was mentioned in the *Century Encyclopedia* a few years after the survey as Mount Sniffles. ❖

Folk Etymology: How We Say It!

What is a picketwire?

With the intermixing of languages in Colorado's past, there have been many transitions in both spellings and pronunciations of place names. As Kim Maurice Swift said in the *Salida Daily Mail* for August 4, 1884:

"This do settle it. The word Salida is pronounced Sa-lee-da, accented on the second syllable and the "i" having the sound of "e," Salida being a Spanish word, meaning 'Gate-way.' (sic) Let us pronounce our own city properly, even if it does at first sound a little dudish."

His own understanding of Spanish was errant, however, as the word salida means "exit." However, his campaign never got anywhere, and if someone were to pronounce the name correctly there today, he would still be considered "a dude." The same with the nearby town of Buena Vista. Instead of proper Spanish, "Bwayna Veesta," people know it simply as "Byoona Vista," or more familiarly as "Byunie." While natives of Pueblo usually get the name straight, outsiders in Colorado often call it "Pee-eb-lo."

The name of the town of Saguache, which is abridged from the Ute word, Sa-gua-gua-chipa, or "water of the blue earth," is called simply Si-watch by the those of European heritage. There is a mountain range, the name of which is pronounced the same way. Why complicate matters? Thus the mountains following the Continental Divide, and including some of the highest in the state, were simplified to the spelling Sawatch.

One of the most remarkable examples of folk etymology in Colorado is the Purgatoire River. It is one of two rivers which were named originally "El Rio de Las Animas Perdidas en Purgatorio, " or "The River of the Souls lost in Purgatory." The name stemmed from a Spanish legend of a troop of Spanish soldiers who disappeared in the area after a murder committed by their lieutenant of their captain. The priests accompanying the unit refused to continue the journey, and returned to Santa Fe. No word was ever heard from the troops again; thus, they were presumed dead without last rites. Their souls were therefore destined to wonder in Purgatory forever.

In the San Juan mountains, the name of the second river of lost souls is now called simply the "Animas," while in southeast Colorado it is "Purgatory." This has given rise to several interesting regional names, such as the town of Las Animas near the Purgatory River, and the Purgatory Ski Area near the Animas River.

When the earliest French trappers arrived at the Purgatory River, they pronounced the word as Purgatoire. Then along came the English-speaking Americans who had a time with the French word, and somehow the result came out to be "picketwire," a common pronunciation of the name today in that region. ❖

The Singing Sands of Alamosa and China

Good old mountain music

Music Pass rises above the Great Sand Dunes National Monument in the San Luis Valley near the city of Alamosa. It got its name from the tunes which emanate from wind blowing among the constantly-shifting dunes. Some of these giant sand piles reach hundreds of feet above the flat floor of the valley.

In an earlier geologic era, the valley was an extension of an ocean. Through time the prevailing westerly winds gradually lifted the sands into piles. The winds rose on the eastern edge of the valley to clear the spectacular Sangre de Cristo mountains which tower overhead, allowing the sand to drop out to the ground below. These mountains were given the Spanish name for "Blood of Christ" in a legend that was told of a dying priest who looked up and saw them turn brilliant red at the setting of the sun. This effect actually happens quite frequently, reflecting on the entire valley below with a crimson hue.

The land-locked sand dune area is unique for its location at least on this continent for it is almost entirely surrounded by high peaks. However, far up the Yellow River in China, there is a similar formation, near the mountain village of Shapotou. As a result of United Nations aid, those dunes have recently been designated as China's first national reserve for desert ecology. ❖

Town Named for a Famous Cartoonist

He gave us the donkey, the elephant and Santa Claus

A bout twenty-seven miles up the Fryingpan River from the town of Basalt, on the old Colorado-Midland Railroad route, is what remains of the town of Nast. At one time, this region was extremely important in transportation, being the connection between booming Leadville and the Western Slope of Colorado through the Busk-Ivanhoe Tunnel beneath the Continental Divide.

The town was named for a man who is possibly the most famous cartoonist in American history, Thomas Nast. The German-born illustrator came to the United States in 1846 at the age of six. Only nine years later, he was on the staff of *Frank Leslie's Illustrated Newspaper* and later served as a cartoonist for *Harper's Weekly*.

What made him most famous, though, were the symbols he devised: a donkey for the Democratic Party and an elephant for the Republicans. Even more than that, he created the American image of how Santa Claus looked, something of an icon even today. His political cartoons were credited with bringing down the infamous Tweed Ring in New York.

Theodore Roosevelt appointed him as the U.S. Consul in Guayaquil, Ecuador, where he died in 1902. ❖

America's Second Biggest Earth Slide

When the Raggeds flowed

While the greatest landslide in the nation's history occurred with the eruption of Mount St. Helens, in Washington, the second greatest ever recorded was in Colorado in 1986.

After several years of greater than usual snowfall and rains, the lower slopes of a range known as The Raggeds, in the West Elk Mountains, began to flow downward. The Raggeds are located between Redstone and Paonia, on the western side of McClure Pass.

This entire formation, about three miles in width, began to flow in early May of that year and continued at the rate of about ten feet a day for more than a month. When the earth slide finally stopped, it had covered the highway below, Colorado 133, with more than forty feet of rock, soil and other debris, including hundreds of trees. The slide dammed Muddy Creek, which flows into the Paonia Reservoir and on to the North Fork of the Gunnison River. Trees which survived along the surface took on a new slant, growing at all sorts of odd angles. These may be viewed in their distorted state even today. Earthquake-like fissures were left on the surface of the slide area.

After equipment was able to open the stream flow, it took more than three months to re-build a rudimentary road over the earth-filled canyon. A new basin had been formed where dead trees still stand, strangled by the inundation. Called the McClure Pass slide, it has been the subject of visits of geologists from all over the world. ❖

Trail City Straddled
the Colorado-Kansas Border

Crossing the line in a saloon

Back in 1883 Kansas lawmakers passed a quarantine law against Texas cattle entering their state in drives to railheads to the East. They feared contamination from possible diseases the cattle might carry, but this action itself threatened the famous cattle drives. The cattlemen, however, realized that Colorado was still open and could lead the cattle to several Union Pacific railroad towns located in Nebraska.

The problem was that farmers in the Arkansas Valley and other waterways of the Colorado Plains had fenced much of the land and were using water sources that were needed for the cattle drives. After much political maneuvering, the cattlemen were able to obtain use of a three-mile strip of land just inside the Colorado border to drive their herds to Ogallala, Nebraska, where the livestock could be loaded and sent on their way.

At the crossing of the Old Santa Fe Trail in Prowers County, just a little east of the present town of Holly, the cattle drivers established a stopping place, the town of Trail City. Trail City was, for a short time, a notoriously wild place. Like most other towns on cattle trails, this stopover was replete with saloons and houses of ill repute. While buildings on the main street faced Colorado, many of the back doors of these same buildings were across the state line in Kansas. Kansas had very strict enforcement against prostitution and had banned the sale of intoxicating beverages.

Several respectable residences were located entirely in Kansas but some saloons straddled the border. In those days, there were no interstate or inter-territorial laws which permitted sheriffs who were pursuing outlaws to go to another state for the arrest. Thus it was quite a simple matter for outlaws who were wanted in either Kansas or Colorado to merely slip out through a building in Trail City and evade arrest.

Some residents of the nearby town of Coolidge, Kansas, were very perturbed by this arrangement. It seemed that hooligans were disturbing the peace when they rode over from the lawless Trail City, Colorado. In due time, the Coolidge denizens took it upon themselves to establish armed guards in and behind those buildings of Trail City which stood in both states.

As fate would have it, Trail City was to survive only for three more years or so. In 1887, cattle prices were caught in a national depression and soon plunged to a point which made the trail drives unprofitable. The National Cattle Trail was soon abandoned. Apparently, there are no remaining buildings on the site. ❖

The Kingdom of Las Animas

A crown made of coal

Citizens of Trinidad, according to historian Barron B. Beshoar, at one time "proudly referred to Las Animas County as the kingdom of King Coal."

Las Animas County, of which Trinidad is the county seat, even had a seal designed which contained a crown for the monarch himself, a piece of coal, a pick and shovel. The wording on the seal was "The Kingdom of Las Animas."

Trinidad took special pride in the fact that the city had been placed under martial law more often than any other city in the United States. It was the center of a number of serious labor disputes upon which the State of Colorado did not look favorably, especially after the powerful John D. Rockefeller took over Pueblo's Colorado Fuel and Iron plant, the main consumer of the coal. It was in Trinidad that Mary Harris, more popularly known as "Mother Jones," came at the age of eighty-two to organize miners for a strike which led to the infamous "Ludlow Massacre."

Called by Rockefeller "the most dangerous woman in America," she helped persuade workers in Las Animas and Huerfano counties to go on strike. She was arrested illegally but was placed in the local hospital so that Denverites would not realize she was under arrest.

Mother Jones kept agitating for labor throughout the nation almost the rest of her life. On her 100th birthday, Rockefeller sent her flowers and acknowledged that she had essentially won the miners' battle. ❖

The Colorado Fjords

A touch of Norway on the Gunnison

The Curecanti Recreation Area, which lies between the towns of Gunnison and Montrose, surrounds three lakes which were the result of three dams built between 1960 and 1976. These dams are all on the Gunnison River. The tallest one, a concrete structure of 496 feet, is near the small settlement of Cimarron.

This dam created a long, very deep and narrow lake named for the dam, Morrow Point. One of the less-publicized attractions in the state is the chance to take a tour on this lake through the Black Canyon of the Gunnison. These motorized tour boats are the only machine-operated craft permitted on the lake.

To take the tour, one must go down (and later return up) a huge stairway deep into the canyon, just below the Blue Mesa Dam. They may then board the boat for a circuit of the lake.

This reservoir still holds much in the way of native wildlife due to its inaccessibility. The walls of the canyon tower hundreds of feet in vertical formations above the narrow passageways. Some tourists who have visited Norway's fabled fjords cannot help expressing their awe at finding strikingly similar formations in the land-locked Colorado area.

All tours are by reservation only with the Curecanti National Recreation Area. ❖

Way Up There in Leadville

Getting higher the higher you get

While it is widely known that Leadville, at 10,200 feet, is the highest incorporated city in the nation, there were a number of mining camps higher than that city which have since disappeared. A number of interesting anecdotes may be told relating to the altitude. This writer was viewing a World War II movie in a Leadville theater. On screen, the bomber squad captain told the crews that, since they were going up to 10,000 feet, they must all wear oxygen masks. The line brought down the house.

It is said that the bartenders can make their supply of alcoholic beverages go twice as far in Leadville, as it is true that one gets "higher" more quickly the higher the altitude. To keep customers sober, more water can be added to their drinks. The stories of mountain men being able to consume great amounts of "Taos Lightnin'" when they came down to Bent's Fort on the Arkansas were more than just fiction. The trappers' blood had adapted to high altitudes and they could sustain more of the potent whiskey at lower elevations.

A study of premature births carried out by the Playtex Foundation in the early 1950s focused on Leadville because it had the nation's highest rate of premature babies (born under five pounds, although full-term). After examining comparative diets, economic factors and other elements which might affect the pregnancy, the study concluded that babies were just born smaller at higher altitudes. The local high school basketball team blamed its losses on that fact, although most of the players had moved in from other places. The host team used to "freak out" visiting teams by having an oxygen tank set up on the opponents' side of the gymnasium.

Actually, biologists have found that almost all forms of life are smaller at higher altitudes, including animals, birds and plants. ❖

Southernmost Glacier in the Nation

Blanca's everlasting ice

Colorado doesn't have many ice fields that last the year around, much less everlasting glaciers. Most of the glaciers that it does have are located in the northern part of the state. The largest of these is Andrews Glacier in Rocky Mountain National Park. There are at least six other glaciers in that park, probably dating back as far as 20,000 years in age. West of Denver, the St. Mary's Glacier is thought to be a remnant of the Ice Age. For many years it was a popular summer skiing location.

It is a bit hard to determine the age of these ice fields, as some which were once considered glaciers did apparently melt almost completely during warm years.

However, there is one in a shaded crevice on the east face of Blanca Peak, in the southern part of Colorado between La Veta and Fort Garland. At a latitude of 37 degrees north, this mountain, 14,345 feet in elevation, is Colorado's fourth highest. The glacier located there is believed to be the southernmost glacier in North America. ❖

Is Colorado a Rectangle?

Making four corners meet

Without going into an argument relative to the curvature of the earth, Colorado's map appears to be a perfect rectangle. It extends from 37 to 41 degrees north latitude, and from 102 degrees one minute to 109 degrees west longitude. But that latter reading is only on the southern boundary! On the north, it pushes out another minute into Utah. Why is this?

A careful look at a map shows a slight shift in the Colorado-Utah line along the west edge of Montrose County. This jog was made in order that the celebrated "Four Corners," the only point in the nation where four states meet, could become just that. The four states are Colorado, Utah, Arizona and New Mexico. They come together at 37 degrees north and 109 degrees west.

Who lost the minute of land: Southern Colorado or most of Utah? How much taxation is involved in that tiny strip along the desert? The decision was probably made back in 1848, with the Treaty of Guadeloupe-Hidalgo, when the United States took Arizona and New Mexico from Mexico. The Latter Day Saints, or Mormons, lost their claim to all regions west of the Continental Divide. No other explanation has been forthcoming, but without the adjustment, the meeting place at the four corners would be about a mile out of whack.

As a result, travelers along U.S. Highway 160, the "Navajo Trail," may pause and have a picture taken with their bodies sprawled over four states at one time yet still in one piece.

There were two other linear errors of tiny consequence. These were both probably surveyors' mistakes. One is a slight shift in the southern boundary south of Pagosa Springs in Archuleta County. The other is on the northern boundary at the edge of Weld County near Hereford. These irregularities are not shown on most maps due to their comparative insignificance. ❖

Peak Name Altered
With Lindbergh's Fall From Grace

Colorado didn't cotton to pro-Nazism

Probably the first full-blown "media hype" in history was the glorification of Charles A. Lindbergh's solo flight across the Atlantic Ocean in 1927. The pilot was again given great attention with his marriage to the famous Ann Morrow two years later. However, the hero and his wife really caught the nation's sympathy when their infant son was kidnapped and murdered in 1932. The press and radio exploitation of that tragedy and the subsequent trial of Richard Bruno Hauptmann, which included such celebrities as Ginger Rogers, was a new level of national publicity development.

Late in the twenties, Coloradans were so infatuated with Lindbergh that they named a mountain in his honor. This peak was at the head of Cascade Creek in what is now the Indian Peaks Wilderness area, about fourteen miles due east of the town of Granby. It is along the Continental Divide and the border between Grand and Boulder counties.

However, when Lindbergh, who was given the epithet "Lone Eagle" by the press, went to Germany to receive a medal from dictator Adolf Hitler, the enthusiasm waned. When he then became a spokesman for the "America First Committee" opposed to war with Germany, and even indicated great sympathy for Nazism, he was much criticized. Though Lindbergh changed his mind when the United States entered World War II, the magic had dissipated.

According to historian and former librarian of Congress Daniel Boorstein in his interesting work, *Hidden History*, "The Lindbergh Beacon atop a Chicago skyscraper was renamed the Palmolive Beacon, and high in the Colorado Rockies Lindbergh Peak was rechristened the noncommittal Lone Eagle Peak." ❖

The World's Largest Flat Top Mountain

"The Mountain of the Sorrel-Colored Faun"

One of the truly beautiful landscapes in the state is that "island in the sky" Grand Mesa, over 10,000 feet high, covered with lush meadows replete with hundreds of different wildflower varieties in the summer. It is also forested and has at least 200 fish-laden lakes on its summit. Claims have been made that this is the largest flat top mountain the world, although that may be hard to prove, considering some formations in South America. The mountain is about thirty miles wide and nearly sixty miles in length.

Grand Mesa was known as Thunder Mountain to the Ute Indians at one time in their tradition and had a number of legends related to it. For one thing it was considered the dwelling place of Ute ancestors. Therefore it was forbidden that the Uncompahgre Utes venture to its summit for any reason except one. Boys who were being initiated into full status in the tribe were sent to the summit, without food or water. These young men were not to eat or drink until they had received a vision from their forebears. Then they could return and relate the vision to their elders. If no such vision was forthcoming, the youth was not to return.

In the original exploration of the region by Escalante and Dominguez in 1776, the priestly wanderers gave it the name "The Mountain of the Sorrel-Colored Faun." The Utes directed them to the summit where they met members of the Laguna Utes from the Salt Lake region who led them on their quest for a route to California. ❖

Tiny Hinsdale County's Remarkable Records

Beware of statistics!

Statistics are notable in their power to create strange, and often distorted, images.

Take as an example the case of Hinsdale County, Colorado. For a greater part of this century, it has held the record as the least populated county in the nation, vying from time to time with Loving County in Texas. In its boom days, the only town in Hinsdale County, Lake City, was reported to have several thousand residents, although that statistic may have referred to the entire mining district.

Notable people from the annals of the West spent time there, including the cigar-chewing gambler, Poker Annie. It was also the location of the first trial of cannibal Alferd Packer, had several lynchings in its records, and yet was the town where the first church in Colorado west of the Continental Divide was built.

In its isolated location, after the mining frenzy died and the mines played out, people left that place which had beautiful scenery but no way to make a living. Three decades ago, the population of the whole county was less than 300.

This status allowed it to have the lowest traffic death rate in the nation until the first fatality occurred. Then, suddenly, it became the county with the highest highway death rate in the nation. The same results were forthcoming in regard to several diseases, in which only one occurrence of diphtheria or typhoid fever caused health statisticians in the nation's capital to view it as an epidemic area.

During recent years, tourists and summer residents have found this isolated mountain spot. While the winter months still have little or no sources of income, the latest estimates of the population have risen to 600, of whom 350 live in Lake City. ❖

Faraway Places
With Strange-sounding Names

From Brimstone Corner to Jesus Canyon

G ranted, many places in Colorado have rather unimagina-tive or repetitious names: Coal Creeks, Sugarloaf Mountains, Dry Creeks, Crystal Creeks and various colored mountains. Others, though, evoke speculation as to their names or elicit fear, delight or a chuckle.

For sheer pleasure, there are Hope Creek in Mineral County, Happy Creek Canyon (Montrose), Oh, Be Joyful Mountain in Gunnison County, Pleasant Valley (Ouray), Good Point in Delta County, Singing Hills (Elbert), Happy Jack Spring in Eagle County, Perfecto Creek (Saguache), and Balm of Giliad Creek in Park County.

There seem to be others that range from scary to downright dismal. Difficult Creek and Troublesome Creek are in Rio Grande and Grand Counties respectively, Disappointment Creek flows through San Miguel County, and Larimer County has Desolation Peaks. Dead Cow Rapids are in Eagle County; Dead Horse Mesa (Montrose); and Deadman Creeks are to be found in Larimer, La Plata and Gunnison Counties. There's a Mad Creek in Routt County; a Poverty Mesa and Calamity Mesa in Montrose County. Starvation Creek (Saguache) is a bit removed from Starvation Point (Montrose). Terror Creek is found in Delta County, where also Hell's Kitchen overlooks Brimstone Corner. Phantom Canyons may be viewed in Teller, Fremont and Larimer Counties, and Baca County has a Skull Canyon. Up in Rocky Mountain National Park is Mummy Mountain, while Terrible Creek and Terrible Mountain are in Montrose and Gunnison Counties. Devil Creek (Archuleta) and Hell Creek (Lincoln and Kit Carson Counties) elicit images such as the Devil's Back Bone in Boulder County. Poison Springs and Creeks are in Montrose, Gunnison, Huerfano, and Saguache Counties. Rattlesnake Canyon is also in Huerfano County, while Stinking Spring Creeks may be found in both Montezuma and Pueblo Counties. For the speculator, Last Dollar Mountain in San Miguel County is a long way from Wallstreet, in Boulder County.

Then there are those places informally named after people: Walt's Corner (Las Animas), Jack's Cabin (Gunnison), Jack's Creek (Saguache), Ted's Place (Larimer), John's Gulch (Teller), Billy Creek (Ouray), Peter's Knob (Montrose), Harry's Creek (Saguache), Roaring Judy Creek (Gunnison), Crazy Woman Gulch (La Plata), Nancy Hanks Gulch (Mesa), Holy Joe Creek (Yuma), and no less than Jesus Canyon in Las Animas County.

Mellow out on Drowsy Water Creek in Grand County, find your fortune in Cloverleaf Valley up in Jackson County, or ponder the origin of Kicking Bird Canal, north of John Martin Reservoir in Bent County. Last of all, consider Evacuation Creek which wanders along the Utah border and into Rio Blanco County. Additionally note that the highway department changed "S.O.B. Hill' in Montrose County to the more pleasant-sounding Blue Mesa. ❖

ABOUT
MUSCULAR
ACHIEVEMENTS

Main Street, Montrose, Colorado, in 1907

Jack Dempsey's First Professional Fight

Kid Blackie vs. The Fighting Blacksmith

One of the greatest heavyweight boxing champions of all time was Jack Dempsey, dubbed "The Manassa Mauler" after his birthplace, Manassa, in the San Luis Valley. His name was really William Harrison "Harry" Dempsey but he adopted the moniker Jack after a famed fighter of a few decades earlier. Harry wasn't the only fighter in the family; his brother Bernie also performed in the ring and he, too, used the name of Jack. In order to prevent confusion, Harry called himself "Kid Blackie' in the early days of his career.

Dempsey's father had a wanderlust, moving the family several times while the children were still young. After living at Creede, Steamboat Springs and Delta, the Dempseys went to Montrose. There, Mrs. Dempsey opened a lunch counter to serve the railroad depot and later the crews digging the Gunnison River Diversion Tunnel, one of the earliest federal reclamation projects in the nation.

Having taken part in several amateur matches in towns such as Telluride, the seventeen-year-old Harry and a friend, Fred Wood, decided in 1912 to stage a match for money. They trained in a carriage works at the corner of South Third and Cascade in Montrose, a building being preserved by the local historical society.

That summer, during the Montrose County Fair, Kid Blackie met Wood, "The Fighting Blacksmith," at a ring they built in the dance hall of the local Moose Lodge. The pugilists sold every ticket printed. After a hard-fought match, Kid Blackie knocked out his friend. The total gate receipts came to about $40 which the two fighters split. This was Jack Dempsey's first professional fight. He later went on to Cripple Creek where he was spotted by a promoter and thence to Salt Lake City and on to the big time. ❖

Founder of Basketball
Won M.D. Degree in Denver

He had planned to be a missionary

James Naismith, an instructor at the International Young Men's Christian Association Training School (now Springfield College), in Springfield, Massachusetts, was concerned in 1891 that there were so few winter athletic sports. In an experiment, he put up two peach baskets on opposite walls in the gymnasium and threw in a soccer ball to play with. He had invented basketball.

A Canadian, his aspiration was to become a medical missionary. He had attained a degree in theology from McGill University in Montreal. Later, he moved to Denver, where he became director of the Y.M.C.A. and enrolled in Gross Medical School, being awarded an M. D. in 1897. During his Denver years, he worked on the game of basket ball, establishing thirteen rules, most of which still stand.

After receiving naturalization papers in Denver, he took a position in 1898 as chairman of the physical education department of the University of Kansas, where he spent the rest of his career. The then-famous inventor of one of the most popular sports in America died in 1939 at the age of seventy-eight. He never did become a missionary, although he wrote later that his aim in life was to "do good." He concluded that encouraging wholesome leisure pursuits among the young would accomplish this adequately. ❖

Anyone For a Game of Cricket?

They even took time out for tea

One of the unsung athletic endeavors in Colorado has been that of the venerable sport of cricket. Granted, it has not been played widely in this state but it has had its moments.

Back when Colorado Springs was referred to as "Little London" because of the popularity of that town among the British, cricket was a rather common pastime. *The Weekly Gazette* of that resort reported in 1888 the formation of "the El Paso Cricket and Tennis Club" which played its first match with a team from Denver. The locals lost but "regarded their defeat as no dishonor," as Denver had some of the nation's best batsmen.

Denver apparently maintained its superior position for several years. In 1871, William Iles, a Britisher, arrived in Colorado Springs and may have started the first team there. When he moved to Denver at the age of sixty-six, he organized a new cricket club in that city and was reported to be playing as late as 1905, at the age of eighty-one.

The only college to field a cricket team was Western State College in Gunnison. From 1968 until 1982, students and faculty there held annual contests. Under the direction of William Edmondson, English historian, they were trained by members of the English speaking Union in Denver. In 1972, the Western State "Mountaineers" went down to defeat before the powerful team from the University of California at Los Angeles.

Today, there are still informal matches held in Denver, and some residents of Montrose and Telluride travel as far as Canada to play. ❖

Colorado's Highest Vertical Climb

A third of a mile straight up

The formidable "Diamond" on the east side of Long's Peak north of Estes Park has long been considered one of the nation's most challenging climbs. It is a sheer formation of a thousand feet and was not conquered until 1960. Dave Rearick and Bob Kamps made the ascent that year. Later, Layton Kor, a famous climber from Boulder, made the first winter ascent.

Colorado's highest vertical climb for those technical experts, however, is not a mountain at all. It is the north face of the Black Canyon of the Gunnison River. There, opposite the Chasm View Point, is a perpendicular stone face at least 1,700 feet in height.

While there had been previous attempts, this stone cliff was not scaled until 1969 by Layton Kor. Most climbers start at the North Rim campground, on the top, and then rappel into the canyon, returning up the same route. This section of the Black Canyon of the Gunnison National Monument reaches a depth of nearly a half mile, but at that point, the climbing face is not quite vertical. ❖

Jumping into Deep Canyons

Dangling death on Serpent's Point

Suicides and threats of suicides seem to be a constant cause of awareness at the Royal Gorge, near Canon City. Perhaps this is because it is spanned by what is believed to be the world's highest bridge, a magnificent suspension structure built in 1929. Workers at the park there are trained to be on the alert for potential jumpers because of the lure of the deep canyon, with the Arkansas River rushing 1053 feet below the center of the bridge.

Strangely enough, the Black Canyon of the Gunnison, on the Western Slope of the Rockies, has not had a verified suicide or proven attempted suicide in recorded history, as of this writing. It is more than twice as deep as the Royal Gorge, as if that would matter to someone wishing to end it all. Less than a quarter of a mile across at the top in one spot, it is more than a half mile straight down to the river. Thus its walls are nearly vertical at some points. One of these is the Serpent Point, the highest technical climbing face in Colorado.

It was not intended as a suicide but five people jumped off Serpent Point on October 10, 1981. Only four reached the bottom of the canyon. These were sky divers from Denver, Oklahoma City and Houston.

It was a calm Saturday morning. These were experienced jumpers, some of whom had dived off a 1,600 foot television tower in Oklahoma. Four men and one woman had decided to make the leap, an illegal activity in the Black Canyon of the Gunnison National Monument. Therefore, their plans had not been publicized, although they had friends watching on both rims of the chasm.

When the first man dived over the edge of this North Rim overlook, he counted to eight, pulled the cord, and sailed smoothly to the floor of the canyon. Then came the second dive, made by twenty-seven-year-old Larry Jackson, of Oklahoma City. Jackson's parachute veered back against the north wall and slid down the stone face 250 feet before becoming snagged on an outcrop. Jackson had hit the wall hard enough to break his back and was dangling helplessly 900 feet above the bottom of the cliff.

This caused the others at the top to hesitate due to the risk, but they decided to go ahead and jump. They drifted by the hapless Jackson, whom they determined was apparently still alive.

Once down at the river, the four realized there was nothing they could do to help their comrade, so they began the arduous trek out of the canyon, arriving at the South Rim campground at about 9:00 P.M. Friends took them into a Montrose motel, where they retired, never informing anyone in authority of the fate of their friend. They later said they did not want to be arrested for their lawless jumps.

It was not until the next morning that someone spotted the poor diver, either still dying or dead, hanging on the so-called Painted Wall beneath Serpent's Point.

When authorities learned of this, they summoned rescue parties from Gunnison and Boulder. The Boulder team brought a thousand foot cable and winch, and the Montrose sheriff ordered a helicopter to make a dangerous descent between the walls, directing climbers down to the site of the victim. Jackson was dead by that time.

On Sunday afternoon, while these efforts were under way, the other jumpers were boarding private airplanes in Montrose to fly home, never having told anyone of the incident. However, authorities had by that time determined what had happened through calls made after Jackson's name and address were found on his parachute. They apprehended the party at the airport. Not only had one man died but also the rescue attempt had cost thousands of dollars in its operation, including irreparable damage to the cable and winch used to bring Jackson's remains to the top of the canyon. The divers were eventually fined $50 for the illegal jump, paying under protest that the rules were not specific as to sky divers. ❖

ABOUT
THE
ARTS

Wild Flower Excursion from Colorado Springs, Colo.
On line of the Colorado Midland Railroad.

Trains used to take passengers high in the mountains for wildflowers

State Song Inspired at Little-Known Pass

The columbine field on Elwood

While it is not heard very often in recent years, the official state song of Colorado, "The Land Where the Columbines Grow," was so designated by the State Assembly in 1915. That was sixteen years before the U. S. Congress voted to make "The Star Spangled Banner" the national anthem.

For decades, the state song was learned by every elementary student. It was often sung each day, especially in rural schools. Some children who learned it had never seen a real columbine. The story of the creation of the song was even more obscured.

Arthur J. Flynn, the first superintendent of the Rio Grande National Forest, was traveling in a spring-wagon from Monte Vista to Pagosa Springs in 1911 with a friend. They were on a road which no longer appears on state maps but can be located at the head of the Alamosa River, in the southwest corner of Rio Grande County, on topographic maps.

Near the summit of Elwood Pass, where the road crosses the Continental Divide, the pair stopped for lunch. Looking over the view, they were stunned by the thrilling sight of a massive field of columbines, the official state flower, in full bloom.

Flynn, who was a former principal in the Alamosa Public Schools, was moved to write a poem about it that evening in Pagosa Springs. He later composed the music for what became the official state song. ❖

Father George's Amazing Leadville Murals

A folk-art Sistine Chapel

He lived to the age of 102, still smoking cigars and drinking coffee and brandy. Father George Trunk, born in Slovenia, read, wrote and spoke seven languages. He was a member of the Slovenia delegation to the peace conference at Versailles following World War I. He wrote translations of books. When German and Italian prisoners of war were held at Camp Hale near Leadville during World War II, he administered mass to each group in its own language, remembering that he had been a prisoner of the Russians in the Balkan upheavals half a century earlier.

It was in Leadville, though, that he left his true memorial. St. Joseph's church in that famous mining town had burned and was rebuilt just before the priest was assigned to that parish. Having visited the Sistine Chapel in Rome, Father George decided that the barren walls and ceiling of St. Joseph's should be decorated with murals.

Although not a trained artist, he knew the folk painting of Slovenia. At the age of sixty-two, he embarked on a project which took two years. It was a depiction of Biblical scenes. As had Michelangelo, he often lay for many hours on a high scaffold to work.

By 1928, Father George had completed the work. It has recently been called the finest example of Slovenian folk art in America; the technique having been long discarded even in the Balkans. His total expense for the materials used came to only $79.

The aging priest served the Leadville parish for a quarter of a century. At eighty-seven, he was assigned to San Francisco and there continued his work in the Church until his death in 1967. His murals still shine from every wall, niches, and the ceiling in St. Joseph's church. ❖

Colorado's Longest-Running Plays

Greater Tuna and Thunder Mountain

When Denver's Stagewest Theater was choosing a play for its inaugural performance in May of 1987, it came up with a real winner. The comedy, *Greater Tuna*, was an immediate hit and eventually ran for 627 performances in Colorado. It then added a fifteen state national tour.

In Denver, the play was performed for eight and a half months in Stagewest's original cabaret-style theater. After that, it moved to the Avenue Theater for another eight-month stint and then returned to its original home, where it packed them in for another eleven months. Thus, *Greater Tuna* holds, as of this writing, the undisputed record as the longest-running play in Colorado history.

As for outdoor theater, the record is held by *Thunder Mountain Lives Tonight!*, an historical production which was performed five nights a week during summers at Delta. It ran for 493 performances between 1986, when it opened, until its final performance in 1995. The original show was changed to a musical during the third season but kept the essential content, a history of the region around Grand Mesa, which overlooks the special arena in which the show was performed. Grand Mesa was known to the Ute Indians as Thunder Mountain, and the Indians from the Southern Ute Reservation took part in the show itself on many occasions. There is some support in Delta for a revival of the play. ❖

Colorado's Unique College Campus

Moscow exhibit prize

In 1962, the town of Rangely in northwest Colorado found itself with enough extra money from taxation of its oil fields to start a junior college. Originally, the college was a branch of Grand Junction's Mesa College, but it is now known as Northwest Colorado Community College. Among its distinctive fields of instruction are aeronautics and dental hygiene.

One has to look twice in order to see the campus on the mesa overlooking the town. It blends into the scenery so as to seem almost invisible.

International acclaim had already been given to the idea of such a campus but no satisfactory location had been found. It was designed by Caudill, Rowlett and Scott, of Houston, Texas. They employed native stone to build the structures and low, slanting roofs to connect to the adobe cliffs on which the buildings were constructed. Tunnels carried all utilities, and walkways between buildings were glassed in to protect the students and faculty against the severe weather, both in the summer and winter, to which Rangely is subject.

At last, there was a real campus in the nation which was a realization of the design which had won top honors at the famous Moscow Exhibition in 1959. ❖

ABOUT

GETTING

AROUND

Laying track on the Kansas Pacific

Strasburg's Claim to the Golden Spike

The first true transcontinental railroad

Much has been written about the driving of the Golden Spike at Promontory Point in Utah. The 1869 event marked the completion of a railroad across the West so that one could travel across the United States entirely by train from coast to coast.

This site has been designated as a national monument. A very tasteful and spectacular dramatic show is seen at the visitor center, climaxed by the curtains parting to show the two locomotives meeting. Many famous paintings and a few photographs celebrate the event. This spot linked the Central Pacific Railroad from San Francisco to the Union Pacific Railroad out of Omaha, Nebraska.

However, it was not truly a transcontinental railroad. As there was no bridge over the Missouri River at Omaha, a passenger would have to cross the river by ferry, leaving one train and continuing on another.

Completion of the first truly transcontinental railroad took place three miles west of the town of Strasburg, in Colorado, on August 15, 1870. There, the road-building crews of the Kansas Pacific Railroad met, with no great fanfare, to form a continuous rail system from coast to coast. Travelers could stay on trains all the way, from east to west. They came by way of Kansas City, bridging the Missouri River there, and continued to Denver, where they could go north to Cheyenne, Wyoming, and on to San Francisco. ❖

Those Dubious Wind-Carts Crossing the Plains

Tacking over the prairie?

There have been a surprising number of stories about sail-equipped vehicles which were supposedly used to carry gold seekers across the plains from the Missouri River to Colorado. One of these was an account in the *Rocky Mountain News* for April 18, 1860. The article related that three men had arrived in Denver in a combination "wind-wagon" and hand-car. They had reportedly made the trip from Missouri in only twenty days. That was better time than taken by most horse teams and the cost of the trip was said to be a masterpiece of economy.

Perhaps it was true, or perhaps not. The trails across Kansas and eastern Colorado were quite narrow. The prevailing winds come from the northwest. This would seem to require considerable large-scale 'tacking' across the ravines and boulder-laden prairie. Thus leaving the trails for long distances and crossing back for other detours seems to be almost an impossibility and certainly could not have accounted for greater total speed in the long run. The vehicles would have had to cover at least twice the miles used by those on the trail. The story must have raised quite a few eyebrows among the other trail-weary arrivals in Denver. ❖

Alphabetical Railroad Stations

From A to P, anyway

When the Missouri Pacific Railroad established a special branch line from Kansas to Pueblo in 1887, the subsidiary was named the Pueblo and State Line Railway Company. Being carried away with an obsessive desire for putting everything into proper sequence, railroad officials decided to name the stations along the route from east to west in alphabetical order, for part of the distance, at any rate. They were even able to use their own names on several of the stops.

Around some of these stations, towns grew up. Some of the stations were later re-named or disappeared completely. The stations, from the Kansas border westward, were: Arden, Brandon, Chivington, Diston, Eads, Fergus, Gleatea, Haswell, Indman, Jolliett, Kilburn, Lolita, Meredith, Nepesta, Olney and Pultney. They were all located in Kiowa, Crowley and Pueblo counties.

Surviving on modern maps, along Colorado State Highway 96, are Brandon, Chivington, Eads, Galatea, Haswell and what is now called Olney Springs.

A famous, or, according to many, infamous name of one of the towns, is that of Chivington, named for the so-called "Fighting Parson," who led a massacre of Cheyenne Indians in 1864. The Indians, under Black Kettle, had been promised that if they went there, they would be protected. The incident remains perhaps the darkest stain on the history of the white man in Colorado. ❖

Automobile Manufacturing in Colorado

Colburns, Fritchles, and the Baker Steamer

According to pioneer auto devotees, there were at least three automobiles that were originally manufactured in Colorado.

In 1909, Denver's Judge E. A. Colburn and his two sons built a number of cars named Colburns. There is no record of exactly how many they produced but apparently the business never gave Oldsmobile any large amount of competition. The two known models were labeled the Rex Atlas and the Skyscraper.

Another automobile made in Denver was the Fritchle, an electric runabout produced by Oliver P. Fritchle. It was made in a garage near downtown Denver. Even less is known about it than the Colburn.

A small factory in Pueblo was where Dr. Hartley O. Baker produced steam-driven cars early in the 1900s. He eventually produced two touring autos, one sports roadster and twenty-two pickup trucks. His model was, he maintained, superior to the famous "Stanley Steamer," as it could go uphill without losing steam and started in seconds, as opposed to having to build up a greater head of steam. ❖

Relocation of Vail Pass

The Monarch refused to change

Charles D. Vail, who headed the highway engineering department for Colorado in the 1930s, was very highly respected. When he did an exemplary job of re-routing the old Monarch Pass, between Salida and Gunnison, the state honored him by re-naming it Vail Pass.

That name did not set well with the residents of that high mountain country. They held such an affection for the traditional name of Monarch that they painted over the new signs which had been erected and restored the name of Monarch. Finally, state officials relented and officially brought back the name of Monarch Pass.

That did not deter the urge of State of Colorado officials to salute this famous man, though. When a new pass was pushed through between Dillon and Minturn, it cut the distance across the state drastically. Prior to that time, automobiles going from Denver to Grand Junction had to veer off over Fremont Pass to Leadville and then over Tennessee Pass and Battle Mountain. Even though this new pass which traversed the Gore Range had only been a dream by Vail, it was appropriately named after him.

Many years later, when the "instant Tyrolean" ski village at the foot of the pass was named for the crossing, Vail's name became famous world-wide. The village became the site of North America's largest skiing resort complex. ❖

When Highways Were Better-Known by Names

You could travel the Rainbow Route

During the first three decades of the twentieth century, when some automobiles had to back over Loveland Pass in order to get proper fuel feed, many Colorado highways were better-known by names than numbers. While perhaps not as efficient as the modern system, the names did carry a flavor of romance and excitement that has somewhat disappeared.

The most significant route through Colorado was the Midland Trail, which ran from Richmond, Virginia, to San Francisco. Because the formidable Continental Divide loomed in this state, the tourist was offered a choice of three routes, none of which was an easy ride. They all involved narrow dirt roads, long distances between service stations, and little maintenance. The guide books simply assumed that no one would travel these routes except during the summer, when rainstorms proved to be the most serious hazards.

A driver could go from Julesburg to Denver, and thence to Grand Junction via either Berthoud Pass or Tennessee Pass (with Battle Mountain) and still would be faced with the narrow defiles of Glenwood and DeBeque canyons, which had only shelf roads. The more popular choice through the state was called the Rainbow Route, which started out of Colorado Springs and went over Cochetopa Pass, through Gunnison to Montrose, and then to Grand Junction. It had fewer uphill grades than the others, although "Son-of-a-Bitch Hill," now known by the innocent name of Blue Mesa, was still a challenge.

What is now U.S. 87 and I-25 from Longmont to Denver was called the Cherokee Trail.

Because it crossed Independence Pass, the route from Leadville to Aspen bore the moniker of the Independence Highway.

The tunneled route from Golden to Central City and Idaho Springs was known as the Prospectors' Trail.

U.S. 40, over Berthoud Pass to Craig and on into Utah, was known as the Victory Highway, commemorating World War I.

The Navajo Trail was the name of U.S. 160 from Walsenburg to the Four Corners and on into Arizona.

From Pueblo to the Wet Mountain Valley was the Gold Belt Highway.

The spectacular drive over Grand Mesa, in Western Colorado, was called both Skyview and Canopy of Heaven.

Of course, some of these have still retained their names, such as Trail Ridge Road through Rocky Mountain National Park, the Million Dollar Highway from Ouray to Silverton, the Chief Ouray Highway from Montrose to Ouray, and the Peak-to-Peak Highway, from Colorado Springs to Estes Park, so-named because it ran from Pike's Peak, just east of Mount Evans, to Long's Peak.

A more recent designation has been the Blue Star Memorial Highway, following U.S. 6 through Colorado. Honoring World War II service men and women, it has not been given much attention since the era of the interstate, and only a few of the markers remain.

The Tenth Mountain Division Memorial Highway crosses Tennessee Pass between Leadville and Minturn, passing the site of Camp Hale, where the famous ski and mountaineering troops were trained.

While not a highway, Skyline Drive above Canon City, built by inmates of the Colorado Penitentiary, is one of the most spectacular paved drives in the state, following the knife-edged formation overlooking the city.

For adventurers with four-wheel drive vehicles there are many daring drives, including the Last Dollar Road out of Telluride and the Oh My God Road (Virginia Canyon) between Idaho Springs and Central City. ❖

The Gallopin' Gosling

Smaller than the famous goose

Many people have marveled over the famed "Gallopin' Goose," the hybrid automotive unit that used to run over the narrow-gauge railway from Ridgway to Telluride and beyond. These "locomotives," which were a cross between a

motor truck and a train, are still on display at Telluride, Dolores, the Colorado Railroad Museum in Golden, and out at Knott's Berry Farm in California.

The Gallopin' Gosling

How did it get its nickname? According to Bruce M. Burbank of Littleton who wrote to Frances Melrose of the *Rocky Mountain News* for her "Rocky Mountain Memories" column, the machines would tend to run hot while climbing the steep grades. To cool off, on the downhill run, the driver would raise the four piece hood, hinged in the center. As speed picked up, the sections would flap like wings, suggesting a goose flying. Another version is that the name came from the way the contraption wobbled down the tracks.

Much less-known, however, is the smaller version of the same combination, which is now located at the Jail House Museum in Silverton. It ran on the Silverton and Northern Railway to places such as Animas Forks and Eureka from 1887 until 1947. Only about eighteen feet in length, it could seat six passengers, or the space could be used for freight. Two household brooms were affixed to sweep the track in front of it. This little machine ran on a regular daily schedule. By extension of the expression, this should be called the "Gallopin' Gosling." ❖

Those Fantastic Colorado Highways

Most follow old burro trails

Colorado's network of highways, spanning the plains and wriggling their way through the mountains, constitutes one of the most complex systems of transportation construction and maintenance in the world.

The longest highway in the state is U.S. 160, snaking its way from the Kansas border to the Four Corners, where Utah, New Mexico and Arizona meet Colorado. The shortest road, seven-tenths of a mile long, is State Highway 187, from downtown Paonia to its meeting with Colorado 133, on the West Elk Scenic Loop.

Colorado's longest highway tunnel is the Eisenhower-Johnson bore, 1.7 miles in length, on I-70. It is interesting that Johnson's name on it has almost been forgotten, although as governor he was a great promoter of the idea of a tunnel underneath the Continental Divide.

The esthetic gem of the system may be the I-70 route over Vail Pass. Its graceful environmental coherence, with cement work tinted to blend with the soil, creates harmony in total design. Careful archeological studies preceding the construction revealed a prehistoric game-processing site, so the highway routing was altered to preserve that region.

From the standpoint of engineering, probably nothing anywhere can match its seventeen miles of I-70 through Glenwood Canyon. With its beautiful sweeping and graciously curving viaducts towering eighty to ninety feet in the air, the stretch has 39 bridges with a combined length of six miles.

The entire project was the last and most expensive in the United States Interstate Highway Program, which began in the late 1950s. This section was completed in 1993, at a cost of nearly a half billion dollars. However, one should keep in mind that the entire project, which won the 1993 Outstanding Achievement Award in engineering, cost only about one-fourth as much as one Stealth bomber. ❖

Colorado's Oldest Operating Hotel

It was once the Hotel Splendide

Serving the public as a hotel almost continuously since 1862 is the Peck House in the town of Empire, also known at one time as the Hotel Splendide.

Built as a private home by New York mining speculator James Peck in 1859, in the first mining boom of what would become Colorado, the house was changed into what was in those days a first-class hotel in 1862.

Among its famous guests were P. T. Barnum, Ulysses S. Grant, William Tecumseh Sherman, astronaut Alan Shepherd and actor Cary Grant. It was owned by Peck descendants for nearly a century and then bought by members of the Coors family of Golden. More recently, it has been owned and operated by Gary and Sally St. Clair. ❖

The Peck House or Hotel Splendide

ABOUT
THE
QUEEN
CITY

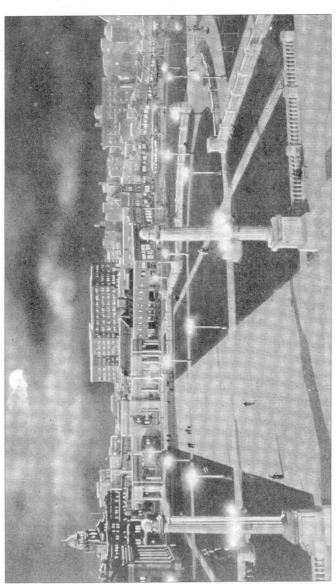

Civic Center at night, from a postcard

The Man Who Lit Up Denver

He also checked up on blackouts

Harold Rankin was the first person to bring colored gels to the United States. These were the filters for flood lights which are so prominent as predecessors for such displays as the Christmas Civic Center lighting in Denver. This son of Colorado pioneers also introduced the first mercury-vapor lights for that city and designed the first flood lights for gas stations in Colorado.

Rankin gained his interest in electrical lighting as a student at the University of Colorado. He was later the head of the commercial lighting department for the Public Service Company of Colorado and was instrumental in introducing neon signs for advertising.

While Rankin brought revolutionary lighting to the city, he was also in charge of blackout regulation for the city during World War II. His airplane inspections of the city at one time found only one house that was showing light, and to his embarrassment, he found it was his own home.

When Harold Rankin died in 1994, at the age of ninety-four, he left a legacy which included many showy theater signs, well-lit streets, and colorful displays to his native city. ❖

Auraria Named for a Georgia Town

It might have been Leather's Ford

After being almost forgotten for a century after its absorption by Denver, Auraria became a prominent name once more as site of the college and university campus along Cherry Creek. The term is the name for "dawn," as it was the first settlement along that stream.

Few people realize that Auraria was named after a town in Georgia that has now almost disappeared. It does not even appear in most road atlases today. At one time, though, it was a booming gold mining center and a challenge to Atlanta in population, according to Georgia historian Olin Jackson.

William Green Russell and his brothers, Levi and Joseph Oliver, were the discoverers of the gold flecks in Cherry Creek in February of 1858. They had been brought up in the village of Leather's Ford, which was located close to Auraria. Foreseeing a great future, they chose the name of Auraria for the crude settlement along the stream.

William was the only one of the brothers who returned to Colorado. After the War Between the States and Sherman's horrible devastation of Georgia, he came out and established a ranch in the Huerfano Valley. Other Georgians joined him in the settlement of that region. A restless sort, though, William later went to the Indian Nation of Oklahoma to live with the Cherokees, to whom he was related by marriage. He stayed there until he died from malarial fever. ❖

Those Kitty-Cornered Streets
In Downtown Denver

Grabbing for the sunshine

Why do the streets in the original part of Denver run in southeast-northwest directions, while the rest of the city is laid out in the traditional north-south, east-west pattern?

According to the late Louisa Arps, noted Denver historian, the original surveyors who laid out East Denver, then known as St. Charles, wanted to do away with the haphazard lack of system in the original cabin alignments. They thought over the plans and studied the climate. That is how they concluded that some portion of each building should be swathed in sunlight for some part of each day.

When Broadway was laid out, Denverites decided that the proper way for streets to run in any city would be the points of the compass. Some historians believe that Henry C. Brown, who built the triangular Brown Palace Hotel, was responsible for that idea. At any rate, with Broadway and Colfax Avenues, the new grid was established. It made for less practical utilization of the sun, especially in the winter. However, with the gigantic buildings of today, that issue is a moot point. ❖

Downtown Denver

Mount Lincoln and Colfax Avenue

Street named for a corrupt veep

Mount Lincoln, towering over Fremont Pass above Leadville, is 14,286 feet in elevation above sea level. It was named for President Abraham Lincoln in 1861 and was at

Schuyler Colfax, after whom Denver's Colfax Avenue was named

that time believed to be the highest peak in Colorado.

Shortly before the President was assassinated four years later, he had sent Speaker of the House of Representatives Schuyler Colfax to Colorado with the mission of thanking the citizens here for the honor.

Coloradans felt so impressed with this gesture at that stage of the War Between the States that they memorialized Colfax by naming Denver's primary east-west artery after him.

Later, however, as Vice President under U.S. Grant, Colfax fell into disgrace as a result of his financial gains in the Credit Moblier scandal. That ended his political career. ❖

Mark Twain and Denver Censorship

Immoral Huckleberry

When the *Denver Post* notified Mark Twain that his book *Huckleberry Finn* had been removed from the Denver Public Library as it was considered immoral, the famous author wrote a letter which was published much later.

In the commentary, Twain remarked, "Huck's morals have stood the strain in Denver and in every English, German and French speaking community in the world — save one — for seventeen years until now ... the strain breaks the connection anew ... in Denver alone ... There's nobody for me to attack in this matter even with soft and gentle ridicule ... and I shouldn't ever think of using a grown-up weapon in this kind of a nursery."

Incidentally, that same book has been withdrawn in many places today for "politically incorrect" language.

As for his knowledge of Colorado, the only place Twain ever visited in this state was Julesburg, which he described as "the strangest, quaintest, funniest frontier town that our untraveled eyes have ever stared at and been astonished with." He made this remark in his book, *Roughing It.* ❖

When Nails Were King

A bonanza after the fire

Denver was swept by fire in 1863, and the conflagration resulted in a financial windfall for young boys. They would find tin cans for containers and poke through the burned ruins of the buildings to find any nails they could rescue for the rebuilding of the Queen City.

Some gathered as many as a hundred pounds or more, getting from five to ten dollars a day for their efforts. That was at a time when very few jobs paid more than a dollar per day, and most wages were lower than that. ❖

Denver's National Party Convention

Bringing down snow in July

Rushed to completion in 1908, Denver's City Auditorium was reported to have a capacity of 10,000. According to Denver historian Tom Noel, it was claimed that this was the largest such building in the nation except for Madison Square Garden in New York City. The cost was reported to be $500,000, an enormous sum for those days.

The reason for the hurry to complete it was that Denver was to hold its only national party convention in its history. The Democratic Party representatives came from all over the nation for the meeting, which nominated for the third time their former candidate, William Jennings Bryan, "The Great Commoner" from Nebraska.

While the convention itself was a bit lackluster, it was a chance for the city to show off, according to the newspapers of the time. Loads of snow were brought down from the mountains to the front of the auditorium, where the convention was assembled from July 7 to 10, giving delegates a good chance to cool off. Indians were there to greet the conventioneers, and the city was decorated with bunting.

Bryan lost decisively to William Howard Taft in the election but later was Secretary of State for Woodrow Wilson, resigning in protest to U.S. entry into World War I. Even later he became famous for serving as the prosecutor in the Tennessee Scopes "Monkey Trial," preserving the right to ban Darwinian Theory from school science classes in that state. ❖

ABOUT

GRAVE

MATTERS

High tea is still served in the Onyx Lobby
of the the Brown Palace Hotel, Denver

The Only Hotel With a Crematorium

Checking out at the Brown Palace

When it opened in 1892, the great Brown Palace Hotel in Denver announced that it had every feature that could be desired by anyone staying in a hotel. Named for Henry C. Brown, who owned the triangular cow pasture on which it was built, the hotel had its own water wells, 700 feet deep.

It offered a private library for guests, a full-sized bowling alley, and billiard tables. Fresh vegetables and dairy products were supplied from the Brown's own farm. In addition to all of these, the amenities apparently included a method for permanent residence. There was a crematorium built into the basement of the building.

There appear to be no records of anyone ever availing himself or herself of this service. Was this actually a section of the heating plant? All that is known about it today is that the crematorium seems to have been eliminated as a result of some remodeling done in 1923.

Perhaps that was the origin of the idea of quick check-out systems. ❖

Don't Trust All Tombstones

Lies engraved in rock

Engraved in stone for all eternity, grave markers are usually considered among the most authoritative sources of
information regarding birth and death dates. However, that is
not always so.

This writer was walking through a very old cemetery at
Leadville with an elderly citizen of that town. Suddenly the
old gentleman remarked that the tombstone was in error. The
deceased whose grave was marked had died three weeks earlier than the stone date, back in 1927. Doubting that one's
memory could span forty years, the writer challenged his
companion, claiming that tombstones don't lie.

Going to the mortuary for a check of the records, though,
proved the gentleman's recollection was correct!

It seems that when tombstones are ordered from afar, the
distraught survivors may forget to mention the actual date of
the death. The engraver then might use the date on which the
order was mailed. When the tombstone arrived, it was much
too costly to have it sent back for correction or to order a new
one, so the imperfect stone was erected. ❖

The Man Who Wore Out His Coffin

Why settle for one funeral?

James Nelson Gernhart, a retired farmer seventy-four years of age at Burlington decided in 1951 that he would have a funeral for himself to see that it was done properly. He scorned his "money-hungry" relatives and was dismayed at the way they skimped on the funeral of his sister. Gernhart, who neither smoked nor drank, had married at the age of fifty-seven but by the time of his first funeral was a widower. Calculating that he had saved enough money through his good habits to afford a proper service, he bought an expensive casket and gravestone, and a plot in the Goodland, Kansas, cemetery, thirty-two miles away, because "I wouldn't be caught dead in Burlington."

The town of Burlington, at first stunned, would have nothing to do with this nonsense, but when he offered to pay the mourners, attitudes changed. A brass band was hired, and the armory was leased. It was reported that nearly a thousand people came to the funeral, or half the population of the town. It was complete with a pre-funeral lunch. Jim loved the experience and the attendant publicity, even making a two-page spread in *Life* magazine.

The next year, Gernhart decided to do the funeral again. Then he began to lie himself in the coffin as a part of the yearly high school homecoming parades. His twenty-fifth anniversary funeral was said to be very spectacular, with a complete re-run of the original, which had been preserved on a wire recorder. He lived to the age of 104, at which time he had upgraded his cemetery plot to a space in a mausoleum. By that time, he had also worn out the original casket and people had worn out their enthusiasm for his funerals. There is no key to the mausoleum at Goodland. May he finally rest in peace. ❖

Two Notable Stray Dog Graves

Shep and Geronimo

At the Broomfield interchange of the erstwhile Boulder Turnpike, there is a fenced gravestone, usually decorated with flowers. This is the resting place of Shep, "part shepherd, mostly affection."

The turnpike was a toll road when it was first opened, and the toll station was located at this intersection. Shep was a stray dog who hung around the station most of his life, which lasted from at least 1950 until his death in 1964. Regular commuters used to bring him treats, and he was shamelessly spoiled by those who worked at the station, where he became a mascot.

Early day lightning express

Not far away, in the Denver Pet Cemetery at Commerce City, there is the grave of one of the most famous dogs in World War II, Geronimo, the paratrooper. Geronimo was believed to be part coyote but mostly German shepherd. He was a stray at Fort Benning, Georgia, in 1942, when he was adopted as a mascot by the 507th Parachute Regiment. One of the soldiers, Ken Williams, became his official master and mentor.

Williams trained Geronimo to jump in a parachute with the troops. It was permitted because dogs could be trained to sniff out explosive charges, which was useful for demolition work. The dog never did get an overseas assignment, although he had made many jumps with the regiment. However, he performed in air shows and was instrumental in helping to sell millions of dollars worth of war bonds.

Geronimo was promoted to sergeant by President Franklin D. Roosevelt, who kept a plaster-of-Paris paw print of the famed canine on his desk. When Ken Williams broke a leg in a jump, he and Geronimo were given honorable discharges.

Ken moved to Colorado to attend the University of Denver in 1943, taking his friend with him. Alas, in 1947, Geronimo was killed by a passing automobile. ❖

An 8,000-Year-Old Mountaineer

Twice the age of Egyptian mummies

Perhaps as long as 11,000 years ago, Ancient Man, or Paleo-Indians, roamed the Great Plains of what is now Colorado. They hunted mammoths whose bones have been found on the prairies. There have also been a few sites in the lower foothills indicative of campsites of those earliest nomads.

These wanderers did not have much in the way of specialized skills or equipment, or so it has been thought.

Recently, though, at a cave whose location is a carefully-kept secret, human remains have been found which appear to be the oldest in any high mountain region. The reason for non-disclosure of the site is to discourage souvenir hunters. The location is over 10,000 feet in elevation, probably somewhere in the San Juan Mountains of southwestern Colorado, a far distance from the Eastern Plains.

Discovered in 1993, the skeleton is that of a male, probably in his late thirties. He had climbed up the mountain and explored a cave there, carrying a torch. It was apparently in the cave that he succumbed to the elements.

This body is twice as old as most Egyptian mummies. It was turned over to the Southern Ute tribe for ritual burial. The Utes, although coming into the area more than eighteen millennia later, are the only extant Native Americans inhabiting the region. ❖

Acknowledgements

The writer is most grateful to the following individuals who gave of their time, wisdom and effort to interviews, suggestions, and commentaries to make this work a reality over the course of the past half century.

Daisy Anderson, Historian, Denver
Cpl. David Batura, State Patrolman, Granby
Roger Blough, County Commissioner, Delta
Mary Louise Fick De Chant, Librarian, Kit Carson
Wallace Dobbins, Journalist, Cedaredge
James DuBois, Technician, Grand Junction
Norman Duensing, Restaurant Owner, Empire
William Edmonson, Historian, Montrose
Gary Eshelman, State Patrolman, Glenwood Springs
Pauline Fikany, Leadville Native, Leadville
David Fishell, Historian, Grand Junction
Alys Freeze, Librarian, Denver
Eleanor M. Gehres, Librarian, Denver
Gordon Hodgin, Businessman, Delta
Stephanie M. Hogan, College Public Relations, Rangely
James and Alice Holme, Colorado Experts, Indian Hills
Evelyn Horn, Botonist, Eckert
Norma Keeler, Librarian, Burlington
Holly Kennedy, StageWest, Denver
Rebecca Lintz, Colorado Historical Society, Denver
Velma McAfoos, Historian, Ouray
Lorie Schilling, Librarian, Granby
P. David Smith, Historian, Ouray
Carl T. Sorrento, Department of Transportation, Denver
Michele Veltri, Historian, Crested Butte
Esther Williams, Historian, Delta
Della Yersin, Librarian, Burlington

Photo Credits

Colorado Historical Society, pp. 46, 54, 66, 80, 98, 146, 156, 162

Collection of P. David Smith, pp. 10, 13, 16, 20, 21, 33, 38, 68, 73, 78, 83, 90, 100, 101, 104, 112, 132, 140, 154, 158, 161, 166, 170

National Farmers Union, p. 30

Books

(Place of publication is Colorado unless otherwise noted.)

Anderson, Daisy. *From Slavery to Affluence.* Steamboat Springs, 1967.

Bailey, Alfred, and Robert Niedrach. *Birds of Colorado.* Denver, 1965.

Baker, Barbara. *Steamy Dreamer: The Saga of Dr. Harley O. Baker.* Grand Junction, 1996.

Bancroft, Caroline. *The Brown Palace in Denver.* Denver, 1955.

Baskin, O.L. *History of the Arkansas Valley, Colorado.* Chicago, Ill., 1881.

Bean, Luther. *Once Upon a Time.* Alamosa, 1975.

Benson, Maxine. *1001 Colorado Place Names.* Lawrence, Kans., 1994.

Beshoar, Baron B. *Out of the Depths: The Story of John R. Lawson, a Labor Leader.* Denver, 1957.

Black, Robert C. *Island in the Rockies: A History of Grand County, Colorado, to 1930.* Boulder, 1969.

Blair, Edward. *Leadville, Colorado's Magic City.* Boulder, 1980.

Boone and Crockett Club. *Colorado's Biggest Bucks and Bulls.* Denver, 1980.

Boorstein, Daniel J. *Hidden History: Exploring Our Secret Past.* New York, N.Y. 1987.

Borneman, Walter R. *Marshall Pass.* Boulder, 1982.

Bright, William. *Colorado Place Names.* Boulder, 1993.

Cairns, Mary Lyons. *Grand Lake in the Olden Days.* Denver, 1971.

Cassells, E. Steve. *The Archeology of Colorado.* Boulder, 1983.

Cassidy, Mary B. *St. Joseph's Church and Parish.* Leadville, 1974.

Century Encyclopedia. New York, N.Y., 1882.

Chrisman, Harry E. *1001 Most-Asked Questions About the American West.* Chicago, Ill., 1982.

———. *The Ladder of Rivers: The Story of I.P. Olive.* Denver, 1962.

Books, continued

Clemens, Samuel (Mark Twain). *Roughing It.* New York, N.Y., 1872.

Clock, Laura. *Cabin and a Clothesline.* Paonia, 1984.

Colorado State Patrol, 1935-1995. (60th Anniversary Commemorative Publication) Denver, 1996.

Davidson, Levette J., and Forrester Blake. *Rocky Mountain Tales.* Norman, Okla., 1947.

DeLorme Mapping. *Colorado Atlas and Gazetteer.* Freeport, Maine., 1991.

Dodge, Grenville Mellen. *Biographical Sketch of James Bridger: Mountaineer, Trapper and Guide.* New York, N.Y., 1905.

Eberhart, Perry. *Ghosts of the Colorado Plains.* Athens, Ohio, 1986.

Erickson, Kenneth, and Albert W. Smith. *Atlas of Colorado.* Boulder, 1985.

Fay, Abbott. *Famous Coloradans.* Paonia, 1990.

———. *Mountain Academia: A History of Western State College of Colorado.* Boulder, 1968.

———. *Ski Tracks in the Rockies.* Evergreen. 1984.

Ferrier, Mamie, and George Sibley. *Long Horns and Short Tales.* Hotchkiss, 1983.

Gear, Ernest. *Eyewitness: Account of the Life of Ernest Gear (1897-1968).* Collbran, 1990.

Gregory, Marvin and P. David Smith. *Mountain Mysteries: The Ouray Odyssey.* Ouray, 1984.

Hafen, LeRoy. *Colorado and Its People.* New York, N.Y., 1948.

Hall, Frank. *History of Colorado.* Chicago, Ill., 1889.

Hassrick, Royal B. *Cowboys and Indians: An Illustrated History.* New York, 1976.

Kaplan, Michael. *Otto Mears, Paradoxical Pathfinder.* Silverton, 1982.

King, A.C. *The Passing of the Storm.* New York, N.Y., 1907.

Lee, W. Storrs. *Colorado: A Literary Chronicle.* New York, N.Y., 1970.

Lindsey, Benjamin, and Harvey O'Higgins. *The Beast.* New York, N.Y., 1910.

Look, Al. *S Fact: 1001 Interesting Facts About the Colorado Plateau.* Grand Junction, 1963.

———. *Sidelights of Colorado History.* Denver, 1976.

Marshall, Thomas Maitland. *Early Records of Gilpin County, Colorado, 1859-1861.* Boulder, 1920.

Melrose, Frances. *Rocky Mountain Memories.* Denver, 1986.

National Midland Trail Association. *The Midland Trail.* Grand Junction, 1916.

Books, continued

Murry, Eerlene Durrant. *Lest We Forget: A Short History of Early Grand Valley, Colorado, Originally Called Parachute, Colorado.* Grand Junction, 1973.

Noel, Thomas, Paul F. Mahoney and Richard E. Stevens. *Historical Atlas of Colorado.* Norman, Okla., 1994.

Olsen, Lee, Ed. *Rocky Mountain Almanac for 1989.* Denver, 1988.

Parsons, Eugene. *The History of Colorado.* Denver, 1917.

Pearl, Richard M. *Colorado Gem Trails and Mineral Guide.* Denver, 1958.

Perkins, James E. *Old Mose: King of the Grizzlies.* Manitou Springs, 1992.

Pratt, John Lowell, and Jim Benagh. *Official Encyclopedia of Sports.* New York, N.Y., 1964.

Rickey, Don Jr. *Forty Miles a Day on Beans and Hay.* Norman, Okla., 1963.

Rinehart, Frederick. *Chronicles of Colorado.* Boulder, 1984.

Rockwell, Wilson. *New Frontier: Saga of the North Fork.* Denver, 1938.

Rose, Ernie. *Utahs of the Rocky Mountains, 1833-1935.* Montrose, 1968.

Ryan, Patrick J. *Twin Lakes.* Leadville, 1943.

Shikes, Robert. *Rocky Mountain Medicine.* Boulder, 1986.

Smiley, Jerome C. *History of Denver, with Outlines of the Rocky Mountain Country.* Denver, 1901.

Smith, Mike. *The Collections of Baldpate Inn.* Estes Park, 1990.

Smith, P. David. *Mountain Mysteries: The Ouray Odyssey.* Ouray, 1984.

———. *Ouray, Chief of the Utes.* Ouray, 1986.

Smith, Toby. *Kid Blackie: Jack Dempsey's Colorado Days.* Ouray, 1987.

Sprague, Marshall. *The Great Gates.* New York, N.Y., 1964.

Stone, Wilbur Fiske, Ed. *History of Colorado.* Chicago, Ill., 1918-1919.

Uchill, Ida Libert. *Pioneers, Peddlers and Tsadikim.* Boulder, 1957.

Wallechinsky, David, and Irving Wallace. *The People's Almanac.* New York, N.Y., 1975.

Willard, Beatrice and Susan Q. Foster. *A Roadside Guide to Rocky Mountain National Park.* Boulder, 1990.

Wilson, D. Ray. *Colorado: Historical Guide Book.* Carpentersville, Ill., 1990.

Wolle, Muriel Sibelle. *Stampede to Timberline.* Boulder, 1949.

Works Project Administration Writers Project. *Colorado: A Guide to the Highest State.* New York, N.Y., 1941. ❖

Articles

Aarps, Louisa. "Downtown Denver Streets." Denver Westerners Roundup. Dec., 1966.

Bangert, Buckley. "Uncompahgre Statesman: The Life of Ouray." Journal of the Western Slope. Spring, 1986.

Bayard, Charles J. "A Notice of Silver Ore in the Upper Platte in 1808." Colorado Magazine. Winter, 1974.

Elmore, Chad. "Colorado's Nearly Forgotten Colburn Automobile." Colorado History News. March, 1996.

Faherty, William B. "Regional Minorities and the Women's Suffrage Struggle." Colorado-Wyoming Academy of Science Journal. Nov. 1956.

Fay, Abbott. "The Battle of the Mining Camps." True West. Spring, 1976.

Fine, Eben C. "The Utes and the Boulder Semi-Centennial Celebration." Colorado Magazine. March, 1939.

Gearhart, Gary. "Nature Watch" columns, Rocky Mountain News. 1989-1996.

Hansen, Diane. "The History of the Roosevelt Windows." (Leaflet) Rifle Public Library, n.d.

Henson, Michael Paul. "Colorado: Mountains of Minerals." Lost Treasure. Dec., 1989.

Jackson, Olin. "Russell-ing Gold in Colorado." Denver Post Empire Magazine. Nov. 24, 1985.

McHendrie, A.W. "Boyhood Recollections of Springfield, Colorado." Colorado Magazine. May, 1944.

Meadow, James. "Lodged In History." Rocky Mountain News. Sept. 18, 1995.

Melrose, Frances. "Rocky Mountain Memories." Rocky Mountain News. March 8, 1995.

Morrison, Martha A. "The School at Bailey, Colorado." Colorado Magazine. Jan., 1941.

Noel, Tom. "Denver Boosters and Their 'Great Braggart City'." Colorado Heritage. Autumn, 1995.

Parkerhill, Forbes. "The Meeker Massacre and Thornburgh Battle: Fact and Fiction." Denver Westerners 1946 Brand Book.

Pearl, Richard M. "Minerals Named for Colorado Men." Colorado Magazine. March, 1941.

Reyher, Ken. "Colorado's Early Hotels." Historian, May, 1997.

Articles, continued

Secrest, Clark. "The 50s: Shake, Rattle and Roll." Colorado Heritage. Winter, 1996.

Slater, Helen. "Yuma." Colorado Magazine. April, 1928.

Smith, Joseph Emerson. "Personal Recollections of Early Denver." Colorado Magazine. Jan., 1943.

Smith, Lynn. "The Early Days of Florence, Colorado." Colorado Magazine. Jan., 1941.

Spencer, Frank. "Colorado State Song." Colorado Magazine. Jan. 1950.

Swift, Kim Maurice. "Pronouncing Salida." Salida Daily Mail. Aug. 4, 1884.

Vaile, Howard T. "Early Years of the Telephone in Colorado." Colorado Magazine. Aug., 1928.

Zingg, Robert Mowry. "The Ute Indians in Historical Relation to the Prot-Azteco-Tenoan Culture." Colorado Magazine. July, 1938.

Author Unidentified Articles

Colorado State Normal School Newsletter. May, 1917.

Grand Junction Daily Sentinel. Sept. 7, 1984, Oct. 3, 1993, Nov. 19, 1994.

Delta County Independent. Aug. 8, 1991.

Durango Daily Herald and Solid Muldoon Souvenir Edition. Jan. 1, 1893.

Johnstown Breeze. July 10, 1924.

Life. Jan. 18, 1951.

Montrose Press. Nov. 9, 1904.

Rico News. Jan-June 1880.

Rocky Mountain News. July 6, 1908; Sept. 4, 1951; Nov. 17, 1994.

Wall Street Journal. Oct. 4, 1991.

Unpublished Manuscripts

Bertelot, Paul Gordon. The History of Creede: A Mining Camp in the Early Days. M.A. Thesis, University of Denver, 1953.

Cohig, Ruth Cowdery. History of Grand County, Colorado. M.A. Thesis, University of Denver, 1939.

Combs, D. Gene. Enslavement of Indians in the San Luis Valley of Colorado. M.A. Thesis, Adams State College, 1970.

Unpublished Manuscripts, continued

Dedman, C.V. The History of Yuma County, Colorado. M.A. Thesis, Colorado State College, (UNC) 1952.

Koplin, Caroly Rand. Colorado's First Struggle for Statehood: Its Relationship to Prevailing Racial Attitudes and Reconstruction Policies. M.A. Thesis, Farleigh Dickenson University, 1972.

Livermore, Charles. James C. Patton: Nineteenth Century Populist, Twentieth Century Organizer, Twenty-First Century Visionary. Ph. D. Dissertation, University of Denver, 1976.

Matthews, Ruth E. A Study of Colorado Place Names. M.A. Thesis, Stanford University, 1940.

Satt, Flora Jane. The Cotopaxi Colony. M.A. Thesis, University of Colorado, 1950.

Weber, Joseph C. The History of the Leadville Public Schools, Leadville, Colorado, From 1877 to 1957. Ed. D. Thesis, Colorado State College of Education (UNC), 1957.

Museums, Libraries and Archives

Adams State College Library, Alamosa
Burlington Public Library, Burlington
Colorado State Archives, Denver
Colorado State Historical Museum, Denver
Delta Public Library, Delta
Denver Museum of Natural History, Denver
Denver Public Library Western History Collection, Denver
Federal Archives Center, Denver
Stephen Hart Library, Colorado Historical Society, Denver
Kit Carson Public Library, Kit Carson
Mesa County Public Library, Grand Junction
Tomilinson Library, Mesa State College, Grand Junction
James Michener Library, University of Northern Colorado, Greeley
Montrose Public Library, Montrose
Museum of Western Colorado, Grand Junction
Ouray and Uintah Indian Reservation Headquarters, Fort Duchesne, Utah
Paonia Public Library, Paonia
Mary Reed Library, University of Denver, Denver
Rifle Public Library, Rifle
Leslie Savage Library, Western State College, Gunnison.

Index

Index, Continued

Index, Continued

Index, Continued